641.6   Olstein, Judi
OL
          Juicing!

$12.98

	DATE	
AP 2 8 '93	FE 01 02	
	SE 26 06	
IV 2 2 '93	JE 25 '08	
FEB 15 '94		
JUN 14 '94	SE 10 '10	
AG 23 '00		
SE 14 '00	8-27-12	
OC 06 '00		
OC 06 '00		
OC 23 '00		
NO 20 '00		
DE 17 '0		

BAKER & TAYLOR BOOKS

JUDI OLSTEIN
JUICING!
PHOTOGRAPHS BY LIONEL MARTINEZ

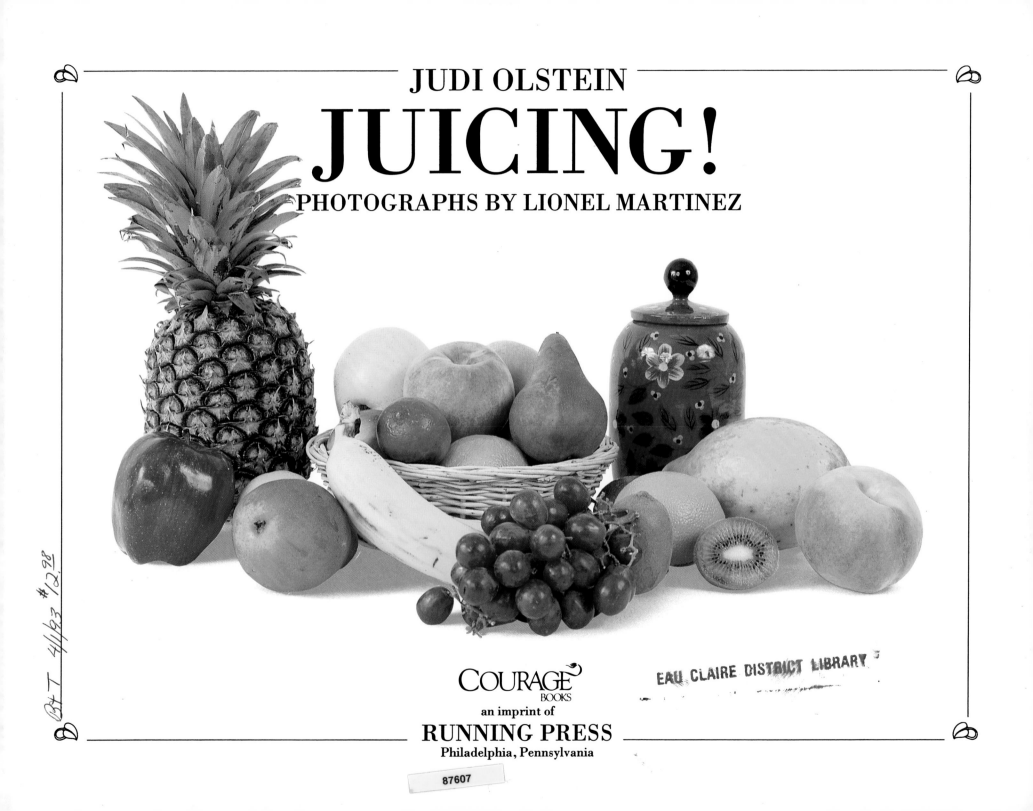

COURAGE
BOOKS
an imprint of
RUNNING PRESS
Philadelphia, Pennsylvania

Canadian representatives: General Publishing Co., Ltd.
30 Lesmill Road
Don Mills, Ontario M3B 2T6.
International representatives: Worldwide Media Services, Inc.
115 East Twenty-third Street
New York, New York 10010.

9 8 7 6 5 4 3 2 1

Digit on the right indicates the number of this printing.

Library of Congress Cataloging-in-Publication Number 92-53811

ISBN 1-56138-184-5

Cover design: Toby Schmidt

Designed and produced by AM Publishing Services and Benford Books
227 Park Avenue
Hoboken, New Jersey 07030
Editorial and Design Director: Tony Meisel
Editor: Barbara Fultz
Art Director: Cassandra Perkins
Photographer: Lionel Martinez
Glassware: D.F. Sanders & Co., 952 Madison Avenue, New York, New York 10021

Published by Courage Books
an imprint of
Running Press Book Publishers
125 South Twenty-second Street
Philadelphia, Pennsylvania 19103

CONTENTS

Freshly juiced tomato and orange juices are a world apart from their counterparts in cans, bottles and cartons.

INTRODUCTION

Juicing is the gateway to good health and fine cuisine, but too often the former takes precedence over the latter. *Juicing!* has been written to bring about a balance, to make healthy foods taste good. By using herbs, spices and flavorings in new and unusual ways, the recipes herein have been devised to add spice and pungency to everyday ingredients.

The juice extractor was born over fifty years ago in a less nutrition-conscious age. Some people bought those early, expensive machines because they felt that there was more to good health than vitamin-enriched breads and cereals. Over the years those pioneers began to grow in number. Before juicers became accepted, certain ideas had to be absorbed by the public. Only in the last ten years have medical authorities found that vitamins, minerals and trace elements have certain disease-preventive properties, and that these can be found most readily in fresh, unprocessed fruits and vegetables. It has also been discovered that vitamin supplements alone cannot supply all the substances needed to maintain good nutrition. As more

and more is unearthed about the role of nutrition in maintaining good health, juicing and its benefits are becoming part of an increasing number of people's everyday diets and lifestyles.

Juicing adds new ingredients and methods to the cook's arsenal. As a number of audacious chefs have shown, juices can be used in place of saturated fats, heavy seasonings and outmoded techniques. Even the pulp left over from the juicing process can be used to enrich sauces, giving body and density to a dish, as well as adding much needed fiber to the diet.

In the following pages you'll find recipes for single- and multiple-juice drinks that will open your eyes to flavor, fresh and singing with vibrant undertones of the fruits and vegetables we too often take for granted.

You'll find "fun" drinks that may just make you forget the coolers, milkshakes and mixed drinks of commerce.

Soups too often come out of a can, but here are recipes for healthful, mouth-watering concoctions that cry out for seconds.

Main courses follow, and they bring new

meaning to the cry of "what's for dinner?" Even using red meats, healthy dishes can be cooked that will add new ammunition to your repertory of dinner centerpieces. Many fish and chicken dishes are quick and easy, and in fact benefit in flavor from the addition of juice and pulp.

Marinades, sauces, dips and dressings bring variety and savor to your meals with little effort, certainly out of proportion to the pleasure received.

Desserts are always a problem for today's lifestyles . . . too rich, too heavy, too fattening. Here are a number of light, delicious fruit desserts and baked goods—cakes, breads and cookies—to satisfy your inner craving for something rich and satisfying. All, however, are moderate in the use of sugar, butter and eggs. They make you feel good and are good for you. Equally, a selection of sorbets will open new doors.

Juicing can be thought of as a way of life, but it can also be considered as an enhancement to an existing lifestyle. In either case, it is new and different, never boring and cause for delicious and healthy eating.

NUTRITION

Juicing is an efficient and pleasant way to give your body the nourishment it needs. Unlike eating raw fruits and vegetables, a glass of healthful juice quickly puts nutritious vitamins and minerals into your bloodstream without having to wait hours for your stomach to digest the cellulose and fiber. Sometimes the normal digestive process misses and even destroys vital nutrients. Juicing can be seen as a predigestive technique that makes maximum use of available vitamins and minerals found in fruits and vegetables.

Several glasses a day of fresh vegetable and fruit juice mixtures provides another important health benefit often overlooked by most people, a continuous replenishment of nutrients lost in normal daily living. According to the former Surgeon General C. W. Koop, "...adequate nutrient and energy intake is critical to the maintenance of optimum immune function."

What is an adequate intake of vitamins and minerals? Anyone with the slightest interest in their own nutritional health has seen the Federal Drug Administration's charts of recommended daily allowances of vitamins and minerals. These charts are based upon the minimum amounts of nutrients needed to prevent vitamin deficiency diseases. Best known of these disorders is scurvy. Scurvy was the bane of ocean-going sailors from the fifteenth to nineteenth centuries. The lack of vitamin C caused this degenerative disease. Early in the nineteenth century, the British learned—even before the discovery of vitamin C—that scurvy could be prevented by including citrus fruits in the sailor's diet. The fruit frequently used by the English was limes, hence the name "Limeys" to signify members of the British navy.

Prevention is an admirable goal, but it does not really address the idea of maximum nutrition. If the recommended daily allowance (RDA) of vitamin and mineral intake is based on preventing disease, what is the optimum daily allowance to insure uninterrupted good health?

An interesting nutritional phenomenon is occurring on America's farms. For over twenty years animal breeders have been feeding their livestock vitamins and minerals five to ten times in excess of the animal's RDA. This is done to ensure that the farmer's livestock will be healthy when the animals are taken to market. In overall terms the herds are remarkably free of disease during their lifetime.

Some medical authorities have attributed this state of well-being to the use of antibiotics in the feed, and not to the use of vitamins. But not all livestock that are fed vitamins are fed antibiotics and they still remain free of disease. Although more research remains to be done in this area, it seems that vitamins are the deciding factor in the livestock's good health.

The vitamins fed to the farm animals are not given in one massive dose, but rather in several large portions at each feeding. The nutrition is spread out during the day, allowing the animals to replenish what each individual needs at the time. What is not needed is eliminated in the urine. Peak levels of nutrition are thus maintained throughout the day.

Sustaining your personal optimum daily

allowance of vitamins and minerals may be necessary to prevent sub-clinical vitamin deficiencies. A growing number of nutritionists believe that the predisposition to various diseases begins at the cellular level with a barely adequate intake of vitamins and minerals. At this degree of nutrition vitamin deficiency diseases are absent, but full nutrition has not been attained. The body's cells receive enough nutrients to maintain minimal life functions. They do not receive enough vitamins and minerals to protect themselves from long-term wear and tear. Eventually the cells die prematurely, the body becomes less resistant to various disorders and some unwanted ailment strikes.

Although this scenario is an oversimplification of complex biochemical processes, it does represent the dangers that some nutritionists believe result from less than optimal nutrition. Sub-clinical deficiencies can be avoided with a continuous supply of vitamins and minerals.

Drinking three to four glasses of fruit and vegetable juices at different times during the day is an excellent way to insure a continuous daily supply of nutrients. In the right combinations it is healthier to have a glass of nutrition-packed juice than to take a vitamin and mineral supplement.

Commercial supplements frequently lack balanced nutrition. In some cases the vitamin pill formula is missing a nutritive helper that enables the body to process important elements. An example would be a vitamin and mineral supplement that contains 10 milligrams of iron, but not enough vitamin C and calcium to aid the body to fully take advantage of the iron. Another problem is that many trace elements and recently discovered nutritive substances are missing from manufactured supplements. Often these nutrients work synergistically with vitamins and minerals by either boosting their value to the body or by aiding in proper metabolism of the substances. Fruits and vegetables often contain many complementary nutrients that help the body metabolize the ingested vitamins and minerals.

It has been known for some time that vitamins have properties that benefit the human body. Beta carotene prevents night blindness. Vitamin C fights hemorrhage and loose teeth. Folic acid helps protect against cervical dysplasia (a precancerous change in the cells of the uterine cervix). These vitamins are most beneficially found in fruits and vegetables and in whole grains.

New research has brought to light the unfortunate fact that many vitamin and mineral supplements are just not up to snuff. A 1989 survey revealed that many supplements on the market are not properly manufactured. Heavily-coated pills are the most difficult to digest, gel caps the easiest.

Additionally, more and more research points to the very real possibility that vitamins, especially those found in fruits, vegetables and grains, may actually prevent or reduce the risk of cancers, heart disease, nerve damage, stoke and muscular degeneration of the eyes in the elderly. Only time and additional studies will establish whether or not this is true, but all the evidence points to good nutrition as a key agent in helping to prevent these scourges of humanity.

Juicing is not only the realm of health-food fanatics, nor is it the answer to all of your nutritional needs. But it is a valuable addition to your effort to maintain good health and may just end up doing far more good than you expected.

Lemon, lime, orange, pear and tomato juices in their rainbow of colors and flavors.

JUICE DRINKS

Most beginning juicers start off with single vegetable and fruit juices.

The most popular vegetable for juicing is the carrot. It produces a milky, orange-colored juice that is like a frothy snack in a glass. A few juicing authorities claim that carrot juice will not keep for any period of time. This is partially true, for the liquid will lose some of its fresh taste several hours after being juiced; but any remaining carrot juice can be used in many cooking recipes, days later, with no discernible loss in carrot taste and little in nutritional value.

This juicing adventure is eagerly continued with celery, apple, orange and tomato juices copiously flowing from the tireless juicer. Once you have tasted these single juices you'll be ready for some simple combinations.

SIMPLE JUICES

Again we must return to the carrot because it is used as a base for many juice drinks. By far the favorite carrot juice combination with both new and experienced juice makers is carrot-orange.

CARROT–ORANGE JUICE

This popular juice is now making its way into the supermarkets as a bottled commercial preparation. It will never match what you can do at home.

2 carrots, washed, lightly scraped, with tops removed
2 oranges, peeled and depithed

Cut the carrots and oranges to fit into the juicer feed tube. Juice and enjoy. Makes 1 glass.
For a snappy change of pace juice a half-inch cube of ginger with the carrots and oranges.

Sometimes a vegetable tasting drink is preferable to a sweet drink like carrot-orange.

CARROT–CELERY JUICE

Another popular juice which can settle a slightly upset stomach due to its celery content.

1 1/2 stalks of celery, washed, with the bitter tops removed
3 carrots, washed, lightly scraped and tops removed

Slice the carrots and celery to fit into the feed tube. Juice. Makes 1 glass. Although this is not a sweet juice, a small cube of ginger would make a great zesty addition on occasion.

CUCUMBER–CELERY JUICE

Cucumbers contain a lot of water and this juice is not as thick as one containing carrots. Don't let its thin appearance fool you. This juice is loaded with vitamins and minerals.

1 cucumber, peeled
3 celery stalks, washed, with the bitter tops
    removed

Put hopper-sized pieces into the juicer and enjoy. Makes 1 glass.

APPLE–CELERY JUICE

2 apples, seeded and cored
2 celery stalks, washed, with the bitter tops
    removed

APPLE–BLUEBERRY

1 apple, seeded and cored
1 pint blueberries, hulled

CARROT–STRING BEAN

2 carrots, washed, lightly scraped, with tops
    removed
1 cup string beans, washed

APPLE–PEAR

1 apple, seeded and cored
1 pear, seeded and cored

COMPLEX JUICES

Juices with three or more ingredients originated in homeopathic and herbal medicine. Many of these recipes were or still are believed to help in building the immune system, cleansing the body or restoring the body's organs. The scientific proof of these claims has been either verified, disproved or not yet examined.

A case in point is the 1992 discovery of the chemical sulforaphane found in broccoli, brussels sprouts and other cruciferous vegetables. This substance was found to stimulate protective enzymes in human cells that protect against the formation of cancerous tumors. But claims made by some juicing advocates for the wondrous powers of vitamin U are completely out-of-line, since vitamin U does not exist.

There may be other chemicals to be found in fruits and vegetables that will be shown to be very beneficial to human health. In the meantime, while we wait for these substances to be discovered, it doesn't hurt to have several glasses of juice each day; it can even be fun!

THE RED V

Your own homemade version of the commercial vegetable cocktail drink. This is also a great all-purpose tonic.

3 tomatoes, washed
2 carrots, washed, lightly scraped, with tops
    removed
3 celery stalks, washed, with the bitter tops
    removed
2 bell peppers, either red or green, seeded
1 cup spinach, washed
1/2 beet, washed
1 clove garlic
1/2 teaspoon lemon juice
salt to taste

Cut all the vegetables into hopper-sized pieces. Bunch up the spinach. Juice. Add the lemon juice and salt. Makes 1 large glass.

EPIDERMAL COMBO

All these ingredients have been said to have a beneficial effect on both hair and skin.

1 cucumber, peeled
1/2 cup parsley, Italian or flat
3 asparagus stalks, washed
1 cup spinach, washed

Slice the cucumber and asparagus into hopper-sized pieces. Bunch up the spinach. Juice. Makes 1 glass.

Carrot juice is loaded with beta-carotene that is really good for your eyes!

Lemon and lime juices combine for a tart and refreshing drink.

COMPLEXION COMBO

Not only is this juice a wonderful skin tonic, it tastes good too. If watercress is not available, substitute an equal amount of parsley.

3 carrots washed, lightly scraped, with tops removed
1 tomato, washed
1/2 cup watercress
1 cucumber, peeled
1 stalk broccoli, washed, tough bottom stalk removed

Cut all the vegetables into hopper-sized pieces. Bunch up the watercress. Juice. Makes 1 large glass.

IMMUNITY SPECIAL I

According to some holistic practitioners this blended juice offers good protection against viral infection.

1 cup blackberries, hulled
1/2-inch cube ginger root, peeled and coarsely chopped
1 cup grapes, red or white, split and seeded
1 carrot, washed, lightly scraped, with top removed
1/2 teaspoon lemon juice

Push the blackberries through the hopper, followed by the ginger root, grapes and carrot. Add the lemon juice. Stir until well mixed and enjoy. Makes 1 glass.

IMMUNITY SPECIAL II

The trace elements found in these vegetables will help to keep your immune system at its best.

3 carrots, washed, lightly scraped, with tops removed
2 broccoli stalks, washed, tough bottom stalks removed
2 asparagus stalks, washed
1 red bell pepper, washed and seeded
1 cup parsley, washed
1 clove garlic

Cut all the vegetables into hopper-sized pieces. Bunch up the parsley. Juice all the ingredients. Makes 1 large glass.

VEGETABLE VIGOR

At present, no juice or miracle substance can make you younger. But you can slow the aging process with a proper diet, exercise and a daily glass of this juice combination. If kale is not available, parsley may be substituted.

1 cup kale, washed
1 cup spinach, washed
2 carrots, washed, lightly scraped, with tops removed
1 cucumber, peeled
1 tomato, washed

Bunch up the kale and spinach. Slice the carrots, cucumber and tomato into hopper-sized pieces. Juice. Makes 1 large glass.

FRUIT VIGOR

A refreshing high energy drink, especially good after an exercise session.

1/2 papaya, seeded
1 cup strawberries
1 cup grapes, red or white, split and seeded
1 orange, peeled and depithed
1 carrot, washed, lightly scraped, with top removed
1 1-inch square ginger root, peeled and coarsely chopped

Scoop out the papaya and juice. Put the strawberries, grapes, orange and carrot into the hopper, continue juicing. Finish juicing with the ginger root square. Stir and enjoy. Makes 1 large glass.

GREEN CLEANSER

Holistic medicine advocates make a strong case for the internal body cleansing properties of many vegetables. Here is a recipe full of these green cleaners.

1 cup cabbage, chopped
1 cucumber, peeled
1 cup parsley, Italian or flat
3 asparagus spears
1 celery stalk, washed, with the bitter tops removed
1 teaspoon lemon juice

Cut all the vegetables into hopper-sized pieces. Juice. Add the lemon juice and stir. Makes 1 large glass.

LIVER CLEANSER

Raw beets have been used traditionally by herbalists as a liver cleanser. Care should be taken not to overdo this recipe; do not use it as part of a daily regimen.

3 beets, washed, tops removed
1 celery stalk, washed, with the bitter tops removed
1/2 cup dandelion greens, washed
1 cup watercress

Cut the beets and celery to fit into the hopper. Bunch up the dandelion greens and watercress. Juice. Makes 1 glass.

MEMORY TONIC

This complex juice can help your memory to be as sharp as any twenty-year old's.

2 stalks broccoli, washed, tough bottom stalks removed
3 carrots, washed, lightly scraped, with tops removed
2 asparagus stalks
1/2 cup parsley
1 1-inch cube ginger root, peeled and coarsely chopped
1 tablespoon kelp powder (available at any health food store)
2 tablespoons almonds, shelled and ground

Cut the vegetables into hopper-sized pieces. Bunch up the parsley. Juice all the vegetables. Transfer the juice to a blender or food processor. Add the kelp and the ground almonds. Blend until well mixed. Pour into a glass. Makes 1 glass.

SLEEP COCKTAIL

Lettuce is a treasured folk tranquilizer and an aid for sleeplessness. Drink this juice a half-hour before bedtime.

3 cups lettuce, any variety, washed
2 stalks celery, washed, with the bitter tops removed
1/2 cucumber, peeled

Bunch up the lettuce and juice. Cut the celery and cucumber into hopper-sized pieces and juice. Pour into a glass and stir. Makes 1 large glass.

AFTERNOON LIFT

Replace that afternoon snack with an invigorating, pick-me-up juice.

3 carrots, scraped, with tops removed
3 celery stalks, washed, with tops removed
1 tomato, cut in quarters
1/2 clove garlic
1 scallion
1 1-inch cube ginger root
2 tablespoons walnuts, ground

Cut the carrots, celery and tomato into hopper-sized pieces. Juice the all the vegetables. Feed the garlic, scallion and ginger root into the hopper and juice. Transfer the juice to a tall glass. Add the walnut powder. Stir. Makes 1 large glass.

*A wide variety of fruits and vegetables can
be combined to make new and exciting juice drinks.*

Juices combining three or more ingredients meld flavors and vitamin benefits.

FUN DRINKS

FRUIT SHAKES

Fruit shakes sprang into being with the invention and consumer distribution of the blender. This class of liquid refreshment was further elaborated on with the advent of the food processor and juice extractor.

Early shakes tended to consist of whatever fruit was available plus the addition of some thickening agent. Both of these ingredients were plopped into the newly purchased blender and processed until they became an homogenized brew. It was soon realized that it was possible to overdo a good a idea. Ten-fruit combinations, tasting like a sweet pulpy mess, were abandoned for more thoughtful mixtures.

Some people call fruit shakes smoothies. The difference is in name only, and the smoothie was so named to put as much distance as possible between the healthy fruit shake and the popular, sugar-and-animal-fat-loaded, milk shake.

Whether they are called smoothies or fruit shakes, these fun drinks share certain common attributes. They are made with fresh fruit and fruit juices. They are thickened with one of the following: yogurt, bananas, milk, ice cream or ice. Extra sweetening is usually added in the form of raw sugar, refined sugar, artificial sweeteners, honey or maple syrup.

Almost any fruit can be used for a fruit shake. If it cannot be juiced, it can be blended into the shake using a blender or food processor. The most common juices for a smoothie are either orange or apple juice. Berries, strawberries, raspberries, blueberries, etc. are the traditional solid fruits.

Fruit shake purists tend to use yogurt, bananas and ice as thickeners. Milk and ice cream are shunned by the faithful. Those with a more laissez-faire attitude will occasionally include those other dairy products in their fruit shakes.

Yogurt produces a thick and tart smoothie. Banana-thickened fruit shakes are heavy and have a sweet tropical taste. When ice is used as a thickener the shake must be consumed before the ice melts. Milk and ice cream will make a shake resemble the diner and luncheonette variety, except that it will contain real fruit.

Refined sugar should be avoided. Artificial sweeteners are just that—artificial. Raw sugar is okay to use, although it will still create the feeling of a "sugar rush" that one gets from refined sugar. Honey and maple syrup are the most popular fruit shake sweeteners, but each of these organic sugars will give the smoothie a distinctive flavor.

What fruit you use and how you thicken and sweeten your fruit shake is up to you. But there is no reason to reinvent the wheel, so here are some time-tested favorites.

SUNRISE SURPRISE

An energy-packed way to start the day when you don't have time for a full breakfast.

5 strawberries, hulls removed
1/2 cup yogurt
1 cup orange juice
2 tablespoons sweetener (your choice)

Put the strawberries and yogurt in a blender or food processor and blend until well mixed. Add the orange juice and sweetener and process again. Serve. Makes 1 tall glass.

RASPBERRY DREAM

A good summer sipping drink.

1/2 cup raspberries
1 cup yogurt
1/2 cup pear juice
1 tablespoon sweetener (your choice)

Blend the raspberries and yogurt in a food processor of blender for 15 seconds. Add the pear juice and sweetener and blend again until well mixed. Makes 1 glass.

BANANA ROYAL

This is a doubly-thick smoothie for those days when you really need a substantial snack.

1 cup orange juice
1/2 cup milk
1 banana
1/2 cup blueberries
1/8 teaspoon nutmeg, ground
1 tablespoon sweetener (your choice)

In a blender or food processor, combine the orange juice, milk and banana. Process until smooth. Add the blueberries, nutmeg and sweetener. Blend until all the ingredients are well mixed. Makes 1 tall glass.

BERRY COOLER

If you love berries then this refreshing fruit shake is for you.

6 strawberries, hulled
1/4 cup raspberries
1/4 blackberries
1 cup pear juice
1 teaspoon sweetener (your choice)
6 ice cubes, crushed

Put the all the berries in a food processor or blender. Process until the berries are puréed. Add the pear juice and sweetener. Blend until the mixture is smooth. Add the ice cubes and give the fruit shake a 10-second burst, or until the liquid is smooth. Makes 1 large glass.

TROPICAL DELIGHT

You don't have to go the Caribbean to have a taste of pristine white beaches on sun drenched islands.

6 strawberries
1/2 mango, peeled and seeded
1 banana
1 1/2 cups orange juice
1 tablespoon sweetener (your choice)
1/2 teaspoon lime juice
1/8 teaspoon fresh mint, chopped

Combine the strawberries, mango, banana and orange juice in a food processor or blender. Process until the mixture is smooth. Add the lime and mint and process once more for about 5 seconds. Makes 2 glasses.

BANANA SMOOTHIE

The perfect alternative to commercially-made thick shakes.

1 1/2 bananas
1 cup yogurt
1/2 cup pear juice
2 tablespoons honey
1/2 teaspoon vanilla

Put the banana, yogurt and pear juice into a blender or food processor. Blend for 20 seconds or until well mixed. Add the honey and vanilla and process for 5 more seconds. Makes 1 large glass.

Peaches add a velvety tang to any juice drink.

With its high water content and natural sweetness, watermelon juices to a perfect cooler.

MELON COCKTAIL

This thirst quencher is to be sipped, not gulped.

1 cup watermelon juice
1 cup raspberries, hulled
1/4 teaspoon lime juice
8 ice cubes, coarsely crushed

Combine the watermelon, raspberries and lime juice in a blender or food processor. Blend until the mixture is smooth. Add the crushed ice and process for 15 seconds. Makes 1 large glass.

EXOTIC PAPAYA

A gift from romantic places, a fruit shake to be shared by two.

1/2 papaya, peeled and seeded
1 banana
1 cup pineapple juice
1/2 cup orange juice
2 tablespoons lemon juice
1 tablespoon sweetener (your choice)
1/8 teaspoon cinnamon, ground

Put the papaya, banana and pineapple juices into a blender or food processor. Process for 10 seconds. Add the orange juice, lemon juice, sweetener and cinnamon. Blend until the mixture is smooth. Makes 2 glasses.

MELON–PEAR NECTAR

Any in-season melon can be substituted in this smoothie.

1 cup cantaloupe cubes
1 cup pear juice
1 tablespoon lime juice
1/2 cup yogurt
1 tablespoon honey
1/8 teaspoon allspice

Combine the cantaloupe cubes, pear juice, lime juice and yogurt in a food processor or blender. Process until the all the ingredients are well mixed. Add the honey and allspice and process once more. Makes 1 tall glass.

TIGER'S MILK

This is not your typical fruit shake. It is a highly nutritious and energizing meal in a glass.

3/4 cup yogurt
3/4 cup orange juice
1 banana
2 strawberries, hulled
5 tablespoons wheat germ
3 tablespoons blackstrap molasses

Pour the yogurt and orange juice into a food processor and blend until smooth. Add the banana and strawberries. Process for 10 seconds. Add the wheat germ and blackstrap molasses. Blend until all the ingredients are well mixed. Makes 2 glasses.

MEXICAN MIX

Some people have claimed that this fruit shake originated in Mexico or parts further south. Its more probable origin is California or parts more trendy.

1 1/2 cups pineapple juice
1/2 cup orange juice
1/4 cup carrot juice
2 tablespoons golden seedless raisins
4 ice cubes, coarsely crushed

Put the pineapple juice, orange juice, carrot juice and raisins in a food processor or blender. Blend until the raisins have almost been pulverized. Add the crushed ice and process for 5 seconds. Makes 1 glass.

OTHER FRUIT DRINKS

ORANGE HEAT

Orange heat is an unusual beverage to be served in the place of an alcohol-based cocktail.

2 cups orange juice
1/4 cup cherry juice
1 tablespoon honey
1/4 teaspoon cayenne, or more to taste
1/2 teaspoon salt

Combine the orange juice, cherry juice, honey, red pepper and salt in a small pitcher. Stir until the honey and salt are dissolved. Makes 2 small glasses.

GINGER TIME

This snappy soda is a good substitution for for an early evening alcoholic beverage.

1/4 cup ginger juice
1/4 cup cherry juice
2 teaspoons lime juice
2 tablespoons sugar
1 1/2 cups cold seltzer
6 ice cubes crushed
2 lime slices

Put the ginger juice, cherry juice, lime juice and sugar in a small pitcher. Stir until the sugar is dissolved. Halve the crushed ice and fill the bottoms of 2 tall glasses. Pour the combined juice into the glasses. Add the seltzer and stir a few times. Garnish with the lime slices. Makes 2 large glasses.

MULLED SUNSHINE

For those cold winter days when you desire a reminder of warmer times.

3 cups pineapple juice
1 cup orange juice
1 cinnamon stick
4 whole cloves
2 tablespoons honey

Put the pineapple juice, orange juice, cinnamon stick, cloves and honey in a medium sauce pan. Bring to a boil and then reduce the heat. Cover and simmer for 20 minutes. Remove the cinnamon and cloves. Serve hot in mugs. Makes 4 servings.

Juice combinations can be served as cocktails.

Mixed berries combine with yogurt for a super smoothie.

SOUTHERN BERRY SODA

If peach fuzz had a taste it would taste like this soda.

1 cup raspberry juice
1 cup peach juice
2 tablespoons honey
1 1/2 cups seltzer
6 ice cubes, crushed

Combine the raspberry juice, peach juice and honey in medium pitcher. Stir until the honey is dissolved. Add the seltzer and stir twice. Halve the crushed ice and fill the bottoms of 2 tall glasses. Pour the juice-seltzer mix into both glasses and serve. Makes 2 large glasses.

CHERRY–LIME RICKEY

This is a minty twist on the old cherry-lime rickey.

1/4 cup lime juice
2 tablespoons lemon juice
1/4 cup cherry juice
3 tablespoons fresh mint leaves, washed and coarsely chopped
2 tablespoons sugar
1 cup seltzer
3 ice cubes

Pour the lime juice, lemon juice and cherry juice into a blender or a food processor. Add the mint leaves and sugar. Blend until the mint has been puréed. Pour the mixture into a large glass and add the seltzer. Stir once. Add the ice cubes and enjoy. Makes 1 tall glass.

SEA BREEZE

An early evening summer sipping soda, especially good by the beach or a lake shore.

1 cup white grape juice
3 tablespoons apple juice
1 cup cold seltzer
6 ice cubes
A few mint sprigs

Combine the grape juice, apple juice and seltzer in a small pitcher. Pour the mixture into 2 glasses. Add 3 ice cubes per glass and garnish with mint sprigs. Makes 2 glasses.

APPLE COOLER

A zippy, refreshing soda that matches an apple's refreshing tartness without upsetting the stomach.

1 cup apple juice
1/4 ginger juice
2 tablespoons lime juice
1 tablespoon sugar
1 1/4 cups cold seltzer
6 ice cubes

Pour the fruit juices into a medium pitcher. Add the sugar and stir until the sugar is dissolved. Add the seltzer and give the mixture two quick stirs. Pour into 2 tall glasses and add 3 ice cubes in each glass. Makes 2 servings.

MELON VERDE

Once a rare and exotic fruit, the kiwi is now found in every supermarket.

1 cup kiwi fruit, peeled and sliced
1 cup white grape juice
1 cup honeydew melon juice
6 ice cubes, coarsely crushed
1/2 cup seltzer

Combine the kiwi fruit, grape juice and melon juice in a food processor or blender. Process until the kiwi is broken up. Add the crushed ice and process until the mixture is smooth. Pour the beverage into 2 tall glasses. Pour 1/4 cup of seltzer into both glasses and stir twice. Makes 2 servings.

SOUPS

A freshly-made soup is the perfect start to a meal. Too often we rely on cans and packets, but juices and other natural ingredients not only add flavor but avoid the chemicals and sodium overdoses of commercially-produced products.

TOMATO SOUP

4 cups tomato juice
2 tablespoons fresh basil leaves, finely
*   chopped*
1 cup plain yogurt
salt and pepper to taste

Combine all ingredients and serve cold. Or heat very gently, stirring constantly, until hot. Do not allow to boil or the yogurt will curdle. Chopped garlic or other vegetables can be added, raw or cooked. If made without the yogurt, the soup can serve as the base for gazpacho. Serves 4.

TOMATO-YOGURT SOUP

A great cold soup for an outdoor dinner starter. For the best results use recently- or just- picked vine ripened tomatoes.

1 pound fresh tomatoes
1 scallion
1/2 cup yogurt
1 tablespoon dried chervil or 2 tablespoons
*   fresh chopped chervil*
several sprigs of fresh parsley
salt and pepper to taste

Wash the tomatoes in hot water to remove any wax. Trim the cores and cut into chunks small enough to fit your juicer. Juice the tomatoes and scallion. Add the juice to a blender. Add the yogurt, chervil, salt and pepper. Blend the ingredients until well mixed. Pour into serving bowls and decorate with one or two sprigs of parsley. Serves 2.

CUCUMBER–YOGURT SOUP

A light, satisfying soup for the hottest of summer days.

2 8-ounce containers plain low-fat yogurt
1/2 cup cucumber juice
1/2 cup cucumber pulp
1 teaspoon chopped garlic
1 teaspoon chopped fresh mint
1/2 teaspoon freshly ground black pepper

Empty the yogurt into a large bowl. Stir in the cucumber juice, pulp, garlic and mint. Let stand, covered, in the refrigerator for 1 hour. Serve in individual cups or bowls, sprinkled with pepper. Serves 4.

Borscht makes an elegant starter from humble ingredients.

Carrot juice and pulp combine
in a rich and tangy soup.

CREAMY CUCUMBER SOUP

A perfect luncheon entree, supplemented perhaps with a slice of just-baked crusty bread.

3 tablespoons unsalted butter
3 tablespoons flour
1 1/2 cups chicken stock or broth
1 1/4 pounds fresh cucumbers
1/2 cup yogurt
1/4 cup fresh chopped dill
salt and pepper to taste

Melt the butter in a small sauce pan. Remove from heat and gradually stir in the flour. When the butter and flour are well mixed slowly add the chicken stock and blend with a whisk. Return the mixture to the stove. Heat, stirring until the broth simmers and is thickened. Remove saucepan from heat and set aside.

Lightly peel the cucumbers to remove any wax. Juice all but one cucumber. Add the cucumber juice and chopped dill to the broth and stir until well blended. Fold in the yogurt. Chop the remaining cucumber into small pieces. Fold into the soup. Chill. Serves 4.

HONEYDEW–PEAR SOUP

A soup which is fine as an appetizer or a light dessert.

1 large honeydew melon
3 ripe pears
2 tablespoons fresh lemon juice
1/2 cup dry white wine
1/8 teaspoon cinnamon
4 sprigs of fresh mint

Cut the melon in half. Remove the seeds and cut the melon from the rind. Slice the melon into juicer-sized pieces and juice. Pour the melon juice into a large mixing bowl.

Peel and core the pears. Chop the pears into small pieces and put into a small heavy saucepan. Add the lemon juice and heat. When the pears boil, reduce the heat and cook for 10-12 minutes, stirring often, until the pears are soft. Pour the warm pear mixture into a food processor or blender and purée. Add the honeydew melon juice and blend. Add the wine and cinnamon and combine with a quick burst of the food processor or blender. Pour the liquid into a serving bowl and chill. Garnish with several mint sprigs. Serves 4.

CARROT–TOMATO SOUP

Its quick and easy and a perfect way to begin a meaty meal.

1 cup tomato juice
1 cup carrot juice
1/2 cup chicken stock
2 teaspoons butter
1 tablespoon fresh parsley, chopped
2 teaspoons scallion, chopped, green part only

Combine the ingredients in a saucepan. Bring to a boil, stirring occasionally. Reduce the heat and simmer for 2 minutes. Serve hot. Makes 2 portions.

GINGER–CARROT SOUP

2 tablespoons vegetable oil
2 tablespoons butter
3 medium onions, chopped
2 cloves garlic, minced
3 cups carrot juice
1 1-inch cube fresh ginger, minced
1 tablespoon soy sauce
3 cups chicken stock
salt and pepper

Heat the oil and melt the butter in a skillet. Add the onions and garlic. Sauté until the onions are transparent. Add the carrot juice and simmer for 30 minutes. Add the ginger and soy sauce and simmer for 20 minutes. Transfer the soup to a food processor or blender and process until the mixture is smooth. Add the chicken stock and blend. Pour the mixture into the skillet and heat until soup begins to bubble. Serves 8.

RASPBERRY–RHUBARB SOUP

Late evening dinners will begin perfectly with this light soup.

2 cups rhubarb, coarsely chopped
1 cup fresh apple juice
1 tablespoon fresh lemon juice
1 cup fresh raspberries
8 tablespoons yogurt

Put the rhubarb and apple juice in a large saucepan. Cover and cook on a low flame for 45 minutes, stirring occasionally. Turn the heat off and allow to cool for 5 minutes. Put the rhubarb-apple mixture in a food processor or blender. Add the raspberries and purée. Pour the soup into a bowl and chill for a few hours. Serve in individual bowls, garnished with 2 tablespoons of yogurt in the middle. Serves 4.

COLD BORSCHT

Cold borscht is an excellent way to introduce a non-juicer to the joys of juicing.

3 beets, quartered, with tops removed
1 cup fresh spinach
1/2 lemon
1 clove garlic
1 hard boiled egg, chopped
1 scallion, green part only, minced

Juice the beets, spinach, lemon and garlic. Pour mixture into two bowls. Sprinkle the the chopped egg and scallion greens on the borscht. Chill for 30 minutes. Serves 2.

Variation: Substitute 1/2 cup yogurt for the hard boiled egg. Swirl the yogurt into the borscht.

CREAMY ASPARAGUS SOUP

On cold spring evenings this makes a delightful soup and tasty way to begin dinner.

3 cups asparagus juice
1/2 cup asparagus pulp
3 eggs, beaten
2 cups half-and-half
2 teaspoons salt
1 tablespoon lemon juice

In a large saucepan, combine the asparagus juice and pulp. Bring the mixture to a boil. Reduce the heat and simmer for 2 minutes. Using a whisk or a fork slowly beat the eggs into the soup. Continue simmering the soup until the eggs are hard. Stir in the half-and-half, salt and lemon juice. Remove from heat and serve immediately. Makes 4 portions.

Cucumber-yogurt soup is cool and refreshing.

Tomato soup can be served hot or cold, thickened with pulp or as a delicate broth.

DIPS AND DRESSINGS

Dips make for easy entertaining or a simple first course. Salad dressings made from scratch bear no relationship or comparison to the viscous, chemical-filled liquids sold in the supermarket.

BROCCOLI DIP

1/2 cup broccoli juice
1/2 cup (4 ounces) cream cheese, softened
1/2 cup (4 ounces) sharp cheddar cheese,
     grated
2 cloves garlic, chopped
2 tablespoons Worcestershire sauce
1/4 cup broccoli flowers, chopped
1/8 teaspoon salt

Put the broccoli juice and cream cheese in a food processor or blender. Process until smooth. Add the cheddar cheese, garlic and Worcestershire sauce. Process again until the cheddar cheese is well distributed throughout the dip. Add the broccoli flowers and salt and blend. Makes 2 cups.

RADISH DIP

Radish dip is a fresh and healthy alternative to using commercially packaged powders.

8 ounces cream cheese, at room temperature
2 tablespoons parsley juice
1 tablespoon scallion juice
1 clove garlic, minced
1 tablespoon fresh dill, minced
     or
1 teaspoon dried dill
1 tablespoon lemon juice
1/2 teaspoon salt
1 cup chopped radishes

Put the cream cheese, parsley and scallion juice in a bowl. Mix, with a spoon, until smooth. Add the rest of the ingredients and mix once more. Refrigerate for half an hour before serving. Makes 2 cups.

SUMMER DIP

1 7-ounce package cream cheese
1/2 cup cucumber pulp
4 radishes, finely chopped
2 tablespoons onion, finely chopped
lemon juice to taste
freshly ground black pepper to taste

Mash cream cheese, thinning with lemon juice. Add the remaining ingredients and whip until smooth. If the dip is too thick, thin with yogurt or milk to desired consistency. Makes 1 cup.

APPLE HARVEST CHUTNEY

A red meat chutney that works especially well with game.

1 1/2 cups apple, peeled, seeded and coarsely chopped
1 cup cantaloupe juice
1/2 cup sweet red pepper juice
3/4 cup onion, chopped
1/4 cup seedless raisins
1/2 cup brown sugar, firmly packed
1/2 cup white vinegar
1 tablespoon fresh red hot pepper, peeled and chopped
2 cloves garlic, minced
1 1-inch cube fresh ginger, minced
1/2 teaspoon salt
1/2 teaspoon cinnamon

Mix all the ingredients in medium saucepan and bring to a boil, stirring occasionally. Lower the heat and simmer for 2 to 3 hours or until the mixture is reduced by half. Remove and refrigerate for an hour before serving. Makes 2 cups.

ICEBERG LETTUCE DRESSING

Lacking flavor of its own, iceberg lettuce can stand up to the heartiest of dressings.

2 tablespoons celery juice
2 tablespoons tomato juice
1 tablespoon scallion, minced
1 clove garlic, minced
1/4 teaspoon paprika
1 tablespoon honey
1/4 cup white wine vinegar
2 drops Tabasco sauce
1 cup olive oil

Combine all the ingredients except the olive oil in a jar with a tight-fitting lid. Shake vigorously for few seconds and let stand for 2 minutes. Add the olive oil and shake until well mixed. Makes 1 1/2 cups.

PEACH–PEAR DRESSING

Ideal for fruit salads. It is also good as a pastry or poached fruit topping.

1 cup peach juice
1 pear, seeded and cored
1 tablespoon lemon juice
1 tablespoon honey
1/8 teaspoon cinnamon

Combine all the ingredients in a food processor. Process until smooth. Transfer the mixture to a saucepan. Cook under low heat until the dressing begins to thicken. Remove and let cool. Serve. Makes 1 3/4 cups.

ASIAN CARROT DRESSING

Not only is the Asian carrot dressing good with green salads, it can be used on steamed vegetables as well. This dressing gets better with age; you can store it in a jar, with tight-fitting lid, for up to one week.

3 tablespoons soy sauce
1/4 cup carrot juice
1 scallion, coarsely chopped
1 clove garlic, coarsely chopped
1 1/2-inch cube ginger root, coarsely chopped
1 cup peanut oil, vegetable oil may be substituted
6 teaspoons rice wine vinegar

Put the soy sauce and carrot juice in a blender or food processor. Process until well mixed. Add the scallion, garlic and ginger root. Process again until the solid ingredients are minced. Slowly add half the oil while the processor or blender is still running. Add the vinegar and the remaining oil. Blend again. Makes 2 cups.

Cucumber dip can be a first course or a cocktail spread.

Dips are perfect with fresh vegetables . . . and healthy, too.

LEMON DRESSING

This tart dressing is best used with such steamed vegetables as asparagus, green peas, broccoli or cauliflower.

1 teaspoon water
1/4 teaspoon salt, or to taste
1/8 teaspoon lemon peel, grated
2 teaspoons dried mint
4 tablespoons lemon juice
1/2 cup olive oil
freshly ground black pepper

Combine the water, salt and lemon peel in a jar with a tight fitting lid. Let stand for 2 minutes. Add the mint and lemon juice, cover and shake. Add the olive oil and black pepper. Cover and shake once more. Serve immediately. Makes 1 cup.

APPLE–BASIL DRESSING

1/2 cup olive oil
1/4 cup apple juice
1 tablespoon fresh basil leaves, chopped
1 tablespoon lemon juice
1/4 teaspoon freshly ground black pepper
1 clove chopped garlic (optional)

Combine all ingredients in a screw-cap jar and shake vigorously until well blended. Let sit for at least 1 hour to give flavors time to meld and develop. Shake again before dressing salad. Makes 1 cup.

ORANGE–CURRY DRESSING

1/2 cup olive or safflower oil
1/4 cup orange juice
1 teaspoon (or more to taste) curry powder
freshly ground black pepper
1 teaspoon onion juice

Combine all ingredients in a screw-cap jar and shake vigorously until well blended. Let sit for at least 1 hour to give flavors time to meld and develop. Shake again before dressing salad. Makes 1 cup.

ZESTY ITALIAN DRESSING

For the best results do not economize—use extra virgin olive oil and balsamic vinegar where called for. This dressing can be stored in the refrigerator for several days.

1 cup celery juice
1 teaspoon dried basil
1/4 teaspoon dried oregano
1/4 teaspoon dried thyme
1/4 teaspoon salt
1 clove garlic, roughly chopped
1 scallion, roughly chopped
1 cup extra virgin olive oil
3 tablespoons balsamic vinegar
2 tablespoons red wine vinegar
1/4 cup regular olive oil

Put the celery juice, basil, oregano, thyme, salt, garlic and scallion in a food processor. Blend until the garlic and scallion are in small pieces. Add half the extra virgin olive oil and process once more for 5 seconds. Pour the remaining extra virgin olive oil into the food processor along with the balsamic vinegar and red wine vinegar. Process until garlic and scallion are minced. Run the food processor again slowly adding the olive oil keep processing for 10 seconds. The last addition of olive oil should thicken the dressing a bit. Makes 2 1/2 cups of dressing.

HERB DRESSING

A great way to enjoy the summer when the lettuce is fresh and your herbs can be picked from the garden. If you plan to use fresh herbs multiply the recipe amount by three.

1/2 cup celery juice
1/2 teaspoon dried chives
1/2 teaspoon dried chervil
1/2 teaspoon dried summer savory
1/2 teaspoon dried basil
1/4 teaspoon salt
1/4 teaspoon freshly ground black pepper
1 scallion, coarsely chopped
1 clove garlic, coarsely chopped
2 sprigs of parsley, coarsely chopped
1 cup extra virgin or regular olive oil
3-4 tablespoons of tarragon vinegar, to taste

Put all the ingredients except the olive oil and vinegar in a food processor. Process until the scallion and garlic are minced. Add half the olive oil and blend. Pour the remaining olive oil and vinegar into the food processor and process until the dressing is well mixed. Makes 2 cups.

*Salads are the natural vehicle for a wide assortment of tangy and healthful dressings.
Many different and unusual greens and other fruits and vegetables
can be combined as an accompaniment to a meal or as the meal itself.*

MAIN COURSES

The main feature of a meal should balance wholesomeness, nutrition and flavor. Following is a selection of unusual, easy-to-prepare main courses which will intrigue and satisfy family and guests.

SHRIMP BOUILLION

1 shallot
1 pound ripe tomatoes, cored
2 pounds large shrimp, shelled and deveined
1/2 cup basil leaves, finely chopped
1 tablespoon lemon juice

Juice the shallot and tomatoes together. In the resulting juice, poach the shrimp for 5 minutes over medium heat. Add the lemon juice and basil and cook 1 minute longer. Serve immediately with rice or pasta. Serves 4.

SOLE WITH CUCUMBER FOOL

A fool is an old English dessert made from stewed, puréed fruit and heavy cream. This fish dish is both light and not sweet, using egg whites and only a touch of cream and cucumber in place of the fruit. It's a perfect dinner entree for warm weather.

4 fillets of sole
white wine
4 egg whites
2 tablespoons heavy cream
2 tablespoons mild, white wine vinegar
1/2 cup cucumber juice
2 shallots finely chopped
2 tablespoons cucumber, peeled, seeded and
finely chopped

Fold the fillets in half and gently poach in half water, half dry white wine to cover. In the meantime, beat the egg whites to light peaks. Boil the shallots and vinegar until reduced almost to an emulsion. Fold the juice, cucumber and shallot mixture gently into the egg whites, along with the heavy cream. Remove the fillets to an oven proof dish. Top each with a few spoonfuls of the egg white mixture, smoothing it out to completely cover the fish. Put under the broiler just until the tops are lightly browned and serve immediately. Serves 4.

SCALLOPS IN RED PEPPER CREAM

A remarkably quick-to-prepare main course. Best made with delicate little bay scallops. Larger sea scallops can be used, but cut them in half crosswise first.

1 clove garlic
2 large, ripe red peppers, cored and seeded
1 pound scallops
1 tablespoon sweet butter
1/4 cup heavy cream

Juice the peppers and garlic together and save the pulp. In a heavy sauté pan, melt the butter and sauté the scallops over medium heat for 2 minutes, tossing lightly. Add the pulp and cook another minute or two. Add the cream and heat through. Serve over rice or couscous. Serves 4.

ORANGE–CARROT TROUT

Whether it is store bought or freshly caught, this juiced recipe puts new life into the ordinary trout.

2 cups orange juice
1 cup carrot juice
1 cup water
3 tablespoons red wine vinegar
1 medium sized onion, sliced
1 teaspoon salt
8 whole peppercorns
2 whole allspice
1 bay leaf
4 parsley sprigs
2 large trout, about 2 pounds each
3 tablespoons butter
1/4 cup shallots, minced
3 tablespoons parsley, chopped
1/2 teaspoon tarragon, dried
salt and pepper to taste
2 tablespoons flour

Bring the orange juice, carrot juice, water, vinegar and onion to a boil in a large skillet. Add the salt. Tie the peppercorns, allspice, bay leaf and parsley in small cheesecloth square and make into a bag. Add the spice bouquet to the skillet and bring to a boil. Lower the heat and simmer for 30 minutes. Add the trout, cover and simmer for about 8 minutes or until the fish begins to flake. Remove the trout and place on a serving platter and keep warm. Remove the spice bouquet from the trout broth and reserve the liquid.

Melt the butter in a small saucepan. Add the shallots, parsley, tarragon, salt and pepper. Stirring constantly, cook the sauce until the shallots are tender. Stir in the flour and cook for 2 more minutes. Raise the heat to medium-high and slowly blend the trout broth into the sauce. Cook the mixture until it begins to boil. Reduce the heat and continue to cook until the sauce thickens. Pour over the trout and serve. 4 servings.

COD FISH STEW

3 tablespoons olive oil
1 onion, chopped
2 cloves garlic
1 cup cucumber juice
1/2 cup white wine
1 tablespoon soy sauce
1/2 teaspoon salt
1 teaspoon dried basil, crushed
    or
1 tablespoon basil, minced
1 bay leaf
2 cups potatoes, cubed
3/4 cup carrots, diced
1 pound fresh or frozen cod fish
1 1/2 cups tomatoes, chopped
1/2 cup mushrooms, sliced
2 tablespoons fresh parsley, chopped
1/4 cup water
2 tablespoons cornstarch
pepper to taste

Heat the olive oil in large saucepan. Add the chopped onion and garlic. Saute until the chopped onion is transparent. Stir in the cucumber juice, white wine, soy sauce, salt, basil, bay leaf, potatoes and carrots. Bring to a boil and cover. Reduce the heat. Simmer for 15-20, or until the vegetables begin to soften. Add the fish, tomatoes, mushrooms and parsley. Cover and simmer until the fish flakes easily with a fork, about 5 minutes.

Remove the fish and vegetables and place on a serving plate. In a bowl, mix the water and cornstarch. Stir in the cornstarch mixture into sauce in the saucepan. Cook until the sauce thickens. Pour the sauce over the fish and vegetables. Serve. Makes 4 portions.

INDIAN PEPPER CHICKEN

A hearty low-fat entree that rivals the best Indian restaurant fare.

1 2-3 pound chicken
1 piece of fresh ginger, 1-inch cube, peeled
    and roughly chopped
5 cloves garlic, chopped
1 large onion, roughly chopped
1/4 cup slivered almonds
1 quart (4 cups) sweet red pepper juice
3 tablespoons Indian curry powder
2 teaspoons ground cumin
cayenne pepper to taste
2 teaspoons salt
1/2 cup vegetable oil
1 cup water
1/4 cup lemon juice

Skin the chicken. Quarter the chicken, separate the wings from the breast, quarter the breast and detach the thighs from the legs. Put the garlic, ginger, onion and almonds in a food processor and process until the onions are well minced. Add the sweet red pepper juice, Indian curry powder, ground cumin, cayenne pepper and salt. Blend until onion is well mixed with the red pepper juice.

Pour the oil into a heavy casserole on top of the stove. Heat the oil on a medium high flame. Add the red pepper mixture and stirring often, fry for about 10 minutes. Preheat the oven to 375 degrees. Stir in the water and lemon juice. Add the chicken. Remove from heat and cover. Place the casserole in the oven. Bake at 375 degrees for 10 minutes, reduce the heat to 350 degrees, stir a few times and bake for 20 minutes. Uncover the casserole and cook for more 10 minutes. Remove casserole and serve with rice. Serves 4.

CHICKEN PARK AVENUE

A tempting casserole dish for a cold winter's night, this can easily and cheaply be stretched to accommodate extra guests.

1 3-4 pound chicken, cut into 8 pieces
    and skinned
1 large onion, roughly chopped
2 cloves garlic, roughly chopped
1/4 pound lean ham, cut into 1/4-inch cubes
1 pound mushrooms, cut in quarters with
    stems
1/2 cup celery juice
1/4 cup carrot juice
1 teaspoon dried or 2 teaspoons fresh
    rosemary
salt and pepper to taste
flour
vegetable oil

Dredge the chicken pieces in flour. In a large, oven-proof pot, brown the chicken until golden over medium-high heat. Remove chicken. Add more oil if necessary and sauté the onion, garlic, mushrooms and ham until lightly browned. Return chicken to pot and mix all ingredients well. Turn down heat to a simmer and add the juices and rosemary. There should be enough liquid to cover the chicken. If there is not, make up the difference with either dry white wine or with dark ale (odd it may sound, but you won't taste the ale and it adds an indescribable richness to the flavor of the finished dish). Season to taste and cook, covered for 1 1/2 hours. Serve over noodles or rice. Serves 4

Marinated, grilled fresh tuna is one of the great treats of the ocean, and is richly satisfying.

CITRUS BARBECUE CHICKEN

A fresh alternative to the same old barbecue sauce.

3/4 cup lemon juice
1 large onion, cut into eighths
4 cloves of garlic
1/2 cup vegetable oil
1 1/2 cups orange juice
1/4 cup soy sauce
2 tablespoons of honey
2 tablespoons of Dijon mustard
1 chicken, cut into moderate sized pieces

Put the lemon juice, onion, and garlic in a food processor. Process the mixture for 15 seconds. Pour in the vegetable oil and orange juice. Process again for 15 seconds. Add the soy sauce, honey and Dijon mustard. Process for last time until the liquid is smoothly textured.

Put the chicken pieces into a plastic bag. Pour in the marinade making sure that all of the chicken is covered. Squeeze the air out the plastic bag and seal. Marinate the chicken for a least a half and hour, but no more than 90 minutes. Remove the chicken from the plastic bag and place a hot barbecue. Turn the chicken after 20 minutes and brush with the remaining marinade. Cook for 20 more minutes or until done. Serves 4-6.

JUICY BEEF STEW

A complete meal in one entree. If there is any stew left over it will taste even better the second time around.

3 tablespoons vegetable oil
2 pounds beef stew meat, cut into 1-inch cubes
1 cup tomato juice
1 cup celery juice
1/2 cup sweet green pepper juice
1 cup beef broth
2 tablespoons red wine vinegar
2 bay leaves
2 teaspoons dried oregano, crushed
2 teaspoons dried basil, crushed
2 cloves garlic, chopped
2 teaspoons salt
1/2 black pepper, ground
3/4 cups cold water
1/2 cup flour
3 cups potatoes, cubed
3 cups tomatoes, coarsely chopped
1 medium onion, thickly sliced
1 1/2 cups green pepper, cored and cut into strips
1 cup carrots, scraped and diced

Heat the oil in a large, heavy casserole. Brown the meat. Add the tomato, celery and pepper juices, vinegar, beef broth, bay leaves, oregano, basil, garlic, salt and pepper. Stir well and bring to a boil. Reduce the heat. Cover and simmer for an hour and fifteen minutes, or until the meat is almost tender. Blend together the water and flour. Uncover the stew and skim off the fat. Stir in the water-flour mixture. Cook until the stew bubbles once more, stirring occasionally. Add the vegetables, stir, cover and simmer for 20-25 minutes or until the meat and vegetables are tender. Serves 8.

ROAST PORK WITH PEACH JUICE

Modern breeding methods have made pork almost as lean as chicken and appreciably lower in fat and cholesterol than beef, lamb or veal. Try this roast for a grand dinner party.

1 3-pound boneless loin of pork, rolled and tied
2 cloves garlic, slivered
1 teaspoon ground coriander
1 teaspoon ground ginger
1 cup peach juice

Make a number of deep incisions in the pork with a sharp knife, inserting slivers of garlic in each. Place the pork in a roasting pan, fat side up in a 350 degree oven. Roast for a total of 1 1/2 hours, turning the heat up to 400 degrees for the last 15 minutes. During the roasting baste with the peach juice combined with the ginger and coriander. The essence of peaches will permeate the meat and a lovely glaze will result. Let the roast stand in a serving platter for 15 minutes before carving. Serve with broccoli, small new potatoes in their skins and a sweet-and-sour chutney or relish in lieu of gravy. Serves 4-6 depending on how substantial other parts of the meal are.

PASTA WITH TUNA SAUCE

An unusual combination, typical of the Ligurian coast of Northern Italy. It makes a fast, delicious meal, accompanied by a salad and dry white wine.

1 pound short, tubular pasta—ziti, penne, etc.
1 cup tomato juice made from Italian plum
    tomatoes
pulp from tomatoes
1 7-ounce can tuna in olive oil
2 cloves garlic, chopped
1/2 cup fresh basil leaves, finely chopped
1 teaspoon capers, roughly chopped

First, make the sauce. Sauté garlic in the oil drained from the tuna. Add the tomato pulp and cook for 2 minutes over medium heat. Add the remaining ingredients and continue cooking for 10 minutes until well-blended and slightly reduced. Cook the pasta in plenty of boiling, salted water until al dente, slightly resistant to the tooth. Drain pasta and immediately place in a large, heated bowl, add the sauce and toss thoroughly. Serve immediately. Serves 4.

ZUCCHINI–HAM AU GRATIN

When served as an entree with a fresh salad, this zucchini ham au gratin is not as heavy as one might think.

1 1/2 pounds ham, cubed
1/2 cup water
1 cup broccoli juice
1 tablespoon lemon juice
4 medium potatoes, thinly sliced
2 medium zucchini, thinly sliced
8 ounces cheddar cheese, grated
1/4 teaspoon black pepper

Put the ham and water in a skillet and brown. Add the broccoli and lemon juice. Stir and heat for a minute. Add the potatoes and zucchini. Cook for 10 minutes or until the zucchini is cooked, but still firm.

Transfer the mixture to a baking dish or oven-proof serving dish. Sprinkle with cheese and pepper. Place the dish in the oven and under the broiler. Broil until the cheese has melted and become slightly brown. Carefully remove the hot serving or baking dish from the oven and let stand for 2 minutes. Serve. Makes 4 servings.
Variation: Substitute 1 cup asparagus juice for 1 cup broccoli juice and 2 1/2 cups fresh asparagus, diced for 2 medium zucchini, thinly sliced.

VEGETARIAN PILAF

2 cups long-grain rice
1/4 cup vegetable oil (olive preferred)
1 onion, chopped
1 carrot, chopped
1 red pepper, peeled, seeded and chopped
1 clove garlic, chopped
1/2 cup almonds or pecans, coarsely chopped
1/4 cup celery juice
2 tablespoons lemon juice

In the oil, sauté the onion, carrot, pepper, garlic and nuts, until the pepper is limp and all are lightly browned. Add the rice and let it take on color for 2 or 3 minutes. Add enough water to cover the rice by one finger. Cover the pot and simmer, stirring occasionally, until the liquid is absorbed. This will depend on the quality and age of the rice. Add the juices, cover and let stand for 5 minutes off the heat. Serves 4-6.

STRING BEAN SALAD

1 pound string beans
1/2 cup tomato juice
1/2 cup tomato pulp
1 large onion, chopped fine
olive oil
vinegar
fresh herbs to taste (chervil, parsley, chives, tarragon are all good ... but use only one or two, please)

Cook string beans in plenty of salted water until just tender and drain. Combine while still warm with remaining ingredients and toss well. Let sit, turning occasionally for at least an hour before serving at room temperature. Serves 4.

Pasta with tuna sauce is an unusual and easy recipe from the Ligurian coast of Italy.

SAUCES AND MARINADES

Marinades and sauces tenderize, enliven and enhance roasts, grills and plain food. Here's a selection of pungent, spicy and herby liquids to make meats and vegetables more interesting.

GREEN SAUCE FOR FISH

5 tablespoons olive oil
1 medium onion, chopped
1 garlic clove, finely chopped
2 cups string bean juice
1 tablespoon lemon juice
1/2 teaspoon salt
1/4-1/2 teaspoon freshly ground black pepper,
*   to taste*

Heat the olive oil in a medium skillet. Add the onion and garlic. Sauté until the onion is transparent. Pour the string bean juice into the skillet and bring to a boil. Reduce the heat and simmer uncovered for 5 minutes. Stir in the lemon juice, salt and pepper. Serve. Makes 2 cups.

STRAWBERRY POULTRY GLAZE

Use this glaze on any poultry from chicken to duck. Next Thanksgiving try it on your turkey.

2 tablespoons olive oil
4 cloves garlic, minced
2 scallions, minced
1 1/2 cups strawberry juice
1/4 cup honey
salt and pepper to taste

Put the olive oil in a medium skillet. Heat and add the scallions and garlic. Sauté until the garlic is just barely brown. Pour the strawberry juice and honey into the skillet. Stir and bring to a boil. Cook over medium heat until the mixture is reduced by half. Stir in the salt and pepper. Makes a little less than 1 cup.

GINGER–LIME–CARROT MARINADE

For best results use this marinade on chicken or pork. The recipe is easily doubled for more than one chicken.

1 1/2 cups carrot juice
1/2 cup lime juice
1 tablespoon salt
3 tablespoons vegetable oil
2 tablespoons honey
1 1-inch square of lime peel, coarsely chopped
1 1-inch cube of ginger root, coarsely chopped

Combine all the ingredients in a food processor or blender. Process until the ginger root almost disappears. Put the chicken, cut into eighths, into a large plastic bag. Add the marinade and squeeze out all the air. Seal the bag. Move the chicken in the sealed bag so that every piece is in contact with the marinade. Marinate at least 30 minutes, but no more than an hour. Follow your favorite broiling or barbecue procedure. Makes 2 1/4 cups.

ORANGE–BEET MARINADE

This marinade is an easy way to perk up your favorite meat stew. It works especially well with pork or lamb.

1/2 cup beet juice
1 cup orange juice
3 tablespoons red wine vinegar
1/2 onion, coarsely chopped
3 tablespoons brown sugar
1 teaspoon salt

Combine the ingredients in food processor or blender. Process until the onions are finely minced. Put the meat, cut into 1-inch cubes, into a large plastic bag. Add the marinade and squeeze out all the air. Seal the bag. Move the meat in the sealed bag so that every piece is in contact with the marinade. Marinate at least 30 minutes, but no more than an hour. Follow your favorite stew recipe. Makes 2 1/4 cups.

FISH STEAK MARINADE

Tuna and swordfish go well with this all-purpose marinade.

1/4 cup lemon juice
1/4 cup lime juice
1 teaspoon dried tarragon, crushed
    or
1 tablespoon fresh tarragon, minced
1 teaspoon Dijon mustard
1 clove garlic, chopped
1/4 cup olive oil

Blend all the ingredients in a food processor or blender until well mixed. Pour the marinade into a shallow baking pan, large enough to hold the fish steak. Put the fish into the shallow baking pan and let marinate for 30 minutes a side. Makes 1 cup.

RED PEPPER–CURRY SAUCE

2 tablespoons vegetable oil
3 tablespoons vegetable pulp, pepper and
    carrot preferred
1 medium onion, finely chopped
1 clove garlic, minced
2 tablespoons red wine vinegar
2 cups red pepper juice
2 teaspoons curry powder
1 tablespoon lemon juice
salt to taste

Heat the oil in a saucepan. Add the vegetable pulp, onion and garlic. Sauté until the onion is transparent. Stir in the vinegar and cook, on medium heat, for a minute. Add the pepper juice and cook for 3 minutes. Add the curry powder, lemon juice and salt. Cook, stirring occasionally, for 5 minutes, Serve. Makes 3 cups.

RED WINE-PEAR MARINADE

1/2 bottle dry red wine
1 large onion, chopped
1 cup pear juice
1 large sprig fresh tarragon

Combine all ingredients in a large glass, enameled or stainless steel bowl. Use as a marinade for lamb or veal. Let meat marinate for at least 2 hours. Pat dry and grill or roast. Makes 2 cups.

Marinades not only tenderize meat, fish and poultry, they add new and complex flavors as well. Note that the tenderer the meat to start, the less marination time is needed.

SPICY MARINARA SAUCE

When using this recipe, remember only vegetable *pulp* should be employed. Pulp containing carrots, celery and leafy greens is the best.

7 tablespoons olive oil, extra virgin preferred
1 large onion, chopped
4 cloves garlic, minced
1 cup vegetable pulp
1 28-ounce can of imported Italian tomatoes, or 2 pounds fresh vine-ripened tomatoes, cores removed, chopped
1 teaspoon dried basil
1 teaspoon dried marjoram
1/2 teaspoon dried thyme
2 tablespoons capers
salt and pepper to taste

Heat the olive oil in a large saucepan. Add the chopped onion and garlic. Sauté on a medium high heat until the chopped onion is soft. Add the pulp and sauté for 2 minutes. Cut up the canned tomatoes and add with whatever sauce is in the can. Reduce the heat to medium and stir in the basil, marjoram and thyme. Partially cover and cook for 5 minutes. Add the capers and cook for another 20 minutes partially covered on a medium low flame.

If you are using fresh tomatoes, follow the instructions as for canned tomatoes except: cook for 10 minutes before adding the capers. Serves 4-6.

BAKING AND DESSERTS

Even baked goods can benefit from juices and pulp. Both add a lightness of flavor and unusual tang to breads, cakes and cookies.

VERY ORANGE COOKIES

1/3 cup butter
1/3 cup shortening
1 cup honey
1 egg, white and yolk
1 tablespoon lemon peel, grated
2/3 cup orange pulp
2 1/4 cups flour
1 teaspoon baking powder
1/2 teaspoon baking soda
1/2 teaspoon salt
1/2 cup fresh orange juice

In a mixing bowl, cream the butter and shortening for a minute. Keep creaming and slowly add small amounts of the honey to the mixture. Blend in the egg, lemon peel and orange pulp. Alternately add, in small batches, the dry ingredients and the orange juice. Continue to cream until the mixture is well-blended.

Chill the dough for half an hour. Preheat the oven to 375 degrees. Remove the dough from the refrigerator and drop teaspoon-sized portions of dough on a greased baking sheet. Place the baking sheet in the oven and bake at 375 degrees for 15 minutes or until the cookies are lightly brown.

APPLE GOODIES

2 cups sifted flour
1 teaspoon baking soda
1/2 cup butter
1 cup brown sugar, packed
1/2 teaspoon salt
1 teaspoon cinnamon
teaspoon ginger
1/2 teaspoon nutmeg
1 egg
1 cup chopped pecans
1 cup finely chopped unpared apple
1 cup mixed dark and light raisins, chopped
1/4 cup apple juice

Preheat oven to 400 degrees. Sift flour with baking soda. Mix butter, brown sugar, salt, cinnamon, ginger, nutmeg and egg until well blended. Stir in half the flour mixture, then the nuts, apple and raisins. Blend in apple juice. Onto greased cookie sheets, drop rounded tablespoons of dough, 2 inches apart. Bake 10 to 15 minutes or until golden. Allow to rest on sheets briefly before removing to cooling racks. Cool completely.

ZUCCHINI–CARROT CAKE

CAKE
2 eggs
1 cup sugar
2/3 cup vegetable oil
1 1/4 cups flour
1 teaspoon baking powder
1 teaspoon baking soda
1 teaspoon cinnamon
1/2 teaspoon salt
1 cup carrot pulp
1 cup zucchini pulp
1 cup chopped nuts

FROSTING

3-ounce package cream cheese, softened
3 tablespoons butter
1 teaspoon vanilla extract
1 cup powdered sugar

Preheat over to 350 degrees. Beat eggs with sugar until frothy. Gradually beat in oil. Add dry ingredients. Beat at high speed for 4 minutes. Stir in carrot, zucchini and nuts. Pour into 9-inch square baking pan. Bake for 35 minutes or until top springs back when lightly touched.
For frosting: In a small bowl blend cream cheese and butter, add sugar and vanilla. Beat until smooth. Spread evenly over cooled cake.

ZUCCHINI BREAD

3 eggs
1 1/2 cups sugar
1 cup vegetable oil
2 cups zucchini pulp
1/2 cup milk
3 teaspoons vanilla extract
3 cups all-purpose flour
1 teaspoon salt
1 teaspoon baking soda
1/4 teaspoon double-acting baking powder
3 teaspoons ground cinnamon
1 cup coarsely chopped walnuts or pecans

Preheat oven to 350 degrees. Beat the eggs until light and foamy. Add the sugar, oil, zucchini and vanilla, and mix lightly but well. Combine flour, milk, salt, soda, and baking powder and cinnamon and add to the egg-zucchini mixture. Stir until well blended, add nuts and pour into 2, 9x5x3-inch, greased loaf pans. Bake for 1 hour or until cake tester comes out clean.

LEMON LOAF

1/2 cup butter
1/2 cup granulated sugar
Rind of one lemon, finely chopped or coarsely grated
2 eggs
1/2 cup lemon juice
2 cups all-purpose flour
3 teaspoons double-acting baking powder
1 teaspoon salt

Preheat oven to 350 degrees. Cream the butter and sugar together, then add the lemon rind and the eggs one at a time, beating well after each is added. Stir in the lemon juice, then sift in dry ingredients gradually. Beat well after each addition until you have a light batter. Pour into a greased and floured 8 x4x2-inch pan and bake for 50 to 60 minutes or until a cake tester comes out clean. Cool in the pan for 10 minutes and then turn out on the rack. Allow to age 1 day before serving.

APPLE–NUT CAKE

1/3 cup butter
1 cup sugar
2 eggs
1 teaspoon vanilla extract
1 1/2 cups all-purpose flour
1 teaspoon baking powder
1 teaspoon baking soda
1 teaspoon salt
1 teaspoon cinnamon
1/2 teaspoon nutmeg
1/2 teaspoon ginger
2 cups apple pulp
1/2 cup apple juice
1/2 cup raisins
3/4 cups chopped walnuts or pecans

Preheat the oven to 350 degrees. Grease and flour an 8-inch square pan. In a large bowl, beat the butter until smooth and creamy. Gradually add the sugar and continue beating until well blended. Add the eggs and vanilla and beat well. Combine the flour, baking powder, baking soda, salt, cinnamon, nutmeg and ginger, and sift them together into the butter-sugar mixture. Beat until smooth and well blended; the mixture will be very stiff. Add the apple pulp, apple juice, raisins, and nuts, beat well. Spread into the prepared pan. Bake for 30 to 35 minutes or until a cake tester comes out clean. Remove from the oven and cool on a rack. Cool completely before serving.

Zucchini bread is tasty and adds fiber to the diet.

ORANGE–CARROT BREAD

6 tablespoons butter
1 cup sugar
1/4 cup honey
1/2 teaspoon cinnamon
1/4 teaspoon nutmeg
1 tablespoon coarsely grated orange peel
1 egg
1 1/4 cups carrot pulp
1/4 cup carrot juice
1/3 cup orange juice
1 1/2 cups all-purpose flour
1 teaspoon baking powder
1 teaspoon baking soda
1/8 teaspoon salt
3/4 cup chopped walnuts or hazelnuts

Preheat oven to 350 degrees. Cream the butter and sugar with a mixer, beating until thoroughly incorporated. Add the honey, cinnamon, nutmeg, orange peel, egg, carrot pulp and juice and orange juice. Thoroughly mix the dry ingredients and the nuts, then blend with the liquid mixture until all the flour is moistened. Turn the batter into a greased 9-inch loaf pan and bake for 1 hour. Let rest in the pan for 15 minutes before turning out on a rack to cool.

STRAWBERRY–APPLE BARS

CRUST
1 3/4 cup flour
2 tablespoons powdered sugar
1/2 cup butter

FILLING
1 cup sugar
1/4 cup flour
1/4 teaspoon salt
6 egg yolks
1 cup heavy cream
2 cups peeled, sliced apples
2 cups apple pulp
1/4 cup apple juice
1 cup sliced strawberries
1/2 teaspoon lemon juice

MERINGUE
6 egg whites
1/2 cup sugar

To make the crust, mix the flour and sugar together. Cut in the butter. Press into a lightly greased 9x13-inch pan. Bake in a preheated oven for 10-12 minutes or until golden. Remove and let cool. Prepare filling.

Toss the sugar, flour and salt together. Lightly beat the egg yolks and cream together, then stir into the sugar mixture. Fold in the apple pulp and apples, apple juice, strawberries and lemon juice. Spread the mixture over the baked crust and bake at 350 degrees for 1 hour or until firm.

Beat the egg whites until foamy. Beat in the sugar, 1 tablespoon at a time, until stiff peaks form. Spread the meringue over the apple-strawberry mixture and bake for an additional 10 to 15 minutes or until lightly browned. Cool thoroughly on a rack before cutting into squares.

BAKED BANANAS WITH STRAWBERRY–LIME GLAZE

4 ripe bananas
1 stick sweet butter
1 pint ripe strawberries
2 limes
sugar or honey to taste

Peel bananas. Melt butter in a flat baking dish. Coat bananas with butter and arrange in dish. Bake 15-20 minutes at 350 degrees until hot through and gently browned. Meanwhile, juice the berries and limes. Combine the juice with one-half the resulting pulp and reduce in a saucepan by half. Add sweetening to taste. Pour over the baked fruit and serve either hot or allow to cool to room temperature. Serves 4.

FRUIT SALAD WITH MANGO SAUCE

A selection of fresh fruits appropriate to the
*   season—bananas, peaches, apples, figs,*
*   plums, cherries, etc.—all cut into medium*
*   size chunks or slices*
1 large mango, very ripe
sugar to taste
1 tablespoon kirsch per serving

Combine all the fruits except the mango in a large bowl. Juice the mango. Combine mango pulp with the juice, sugar to taste and the kirsch and whirl a few seconds in a blender. Pour over the fruits and let macerate for an hour before serving.

Apple-nut cake.

SORBETS

Almost any of the single, double or fun drinks can be made into a sorbet. The secret is in the freezing. After making the juice, pour the mixture into a ice cube freezer tray. Freeze until almost solid. Remove the cubes and put into a food processor or blender. At this point one or more liquid ingredients may be added. *The one important ingredient that must be added at this stage is one egg white.* Process until the cubes have become a thick slush. Return the mixture to the freezer and freeze until the desired texture, soft or firm, is obtained.

PEAR–AMARETTO SORBET

A sweet yet delicate sorbet for an evening by the fireplace.

2 1/2 cups pear juice
3 tablespoons sugar
1/2 cup water
2 tablespoons lime juice
1 egg white
3 tablespoons Amaretto

Put the pear juice, sugar, water and lime juice in a large jar with a tight fitting lid. Shake or stir until the sugar is dissolved. Pour into a freezer ice cube tray. Freeze until almost solid. Remove the cubes and put into a food processor or blender. Add the egg white and Amaretto. Process until the cubes have become a thick slush. Pour the sorbet into a bowl and return the mixture to the freezer. Freeze until the desired texture is obtained. Makes 6 servings.

ORANGE–MINT VODKA SORBET

A popular cocktail is now an after-dinner dessert.

2 cups orange juice
1/2 cup water
3 tablespoons fresh mint, chopped
3 tablespoons sugar
1 tablespoon lemon juice
1 egg white
1/3 cup vodka

Put the orange juice, water, mint, sugar and lemon juice in a food processor or blender. Process until the mint leaves are tiny little flecks. Pour into a freezer ice cube tray. Freeze until almost solid. Remove the cubes and put into a food processor or blender. Add the egg white and vodka. Process until the cubes have become a thick slush. Pour the sorbet into a bowl and return the mixture to the freezer. Freeze until the desired texture is obtained. Makes 6 servings.

MELON–GO–ROUND

A perfect summer treat, when the melons are ripe and the living is easy.

1 cup watermelon juice
1 cup honeydew juice
5 strawberries, hulled and frozen
1/4 cup honey
1/4 teaspoon nutmeg
1 egg white

Combine the watermelon juice, honeydew juice, strawberries, honey and nutmeg in a food processor or blender. Process until the strawberries are minced. Pour the mixture into an ice cube tray. Freeze. Remove the cubes and put into a food processor or blender. Add the egg white and process until the mixture is soft. Pour the sorbet into a bowl and return the mixture to the freezer. Freeze until the sorbet is firm. Makes 6 servings.

TANGY GRAPE

Not your ordinary grape sorbet. The tartness of this dessert makes it a perfect end to a rich dinner.

1 1/4 cups green seedless grape juice
1/4 cup lime juice
1/2 cup water
3 tablespoons sugar
1 egg white

Put the grape juice, lime juice, water and sugar in a large jar with a tight-fitting lid. Shake or stir until the sugar is dissolved. Pour into a ice cube tray. Freeze. Remove the cubes from the tray and put into a food processor or blender. Add the egg white and process until the mixture becomes slushy. Pour the sorbet into a bowl and return the mixture to the freezer. The sorbet is ready when the mixture has frozen to a firm texture. Makes 6 portions.

APPLE–BLUEBERRY CREAM

When is a pie not a pie?—when it is an apple-blueberry cream sorbet!

1 1/4 cups apple juice
1 cup blueberries
1/2 cup water
1/2 teaspoon cinnamon, ground
3 tablespoons honey
3 tablespoons heavy cream

Combine the apple juice, blueberries, water and cinnamon in a food processor or blender. Process until the blueberries are minced. Pour the mixture into an ice cube tray. Freeze. Remove the cubes and put into a food processor or blender. Add the honey and cream. Blend until the mixture is thick. Pour the sorbet into a bowl and return the mixture to the freezer. Freeze until the sorbet is firm. Serves 6.

RASPBERRY COOLER

The ideal accompaniment for a lawn picnic.

1 1/2 cups white wine
1 cup raspberries, washed
2 tablespoons sugar
1/4 cup water
1 tablespoon brandy

Combine the wine and raspberries in a food processor or blender. Process until the raspberries are minced. Add the sugar, water and brandy. Process again and pour the liquid into an ice cube tray. Freeze until the cubes are almost hard. Remove the cubes and put into a food processor or blender. Blend until the mixture is thick. Pour the sorbet into a bowl and return the mixture to the freezer. Freeze until the desired texture, soft or firm, is obtained. Serves 6.

APPLE–APRICOT SORBET

This sorbet makes a great autumn dessert.

1 cup apple juice
2 cups apricots, halved and pitted
3 tablespoons sugar
1/8 teaspoon allspice
1/2 cup water
1 tablespoon lemon juice
1 egg white

Combine all the ingredients except the egg white in a food processor or blender. Process until the apricots have fully mixed with the apple juice. Pour into a ice cube tray. Freeze. Remove the cubes from the tray and put into a food processor or blender. Add the egg white and process until the mixture becomes slushy. Pour the sorbet into a bowl and return the mixture to the freezer. The sorbet is ready when the mixture has frozen to a firm texture. Makes 6 portions.

MANGO–PEAR SORBET

Bright and tasty treat that kids from nine to ninety will adore.

2 cups mangoes, peeled, seeded and cubed
1 1/4 cups pear juice
1/2 cup water
3 tablespoons sugar
1 tablespoon lemon juice
1/4 cup heavy cream

In a food processor or blender, put the mangoes, pear juice, water, sugar and lemon juice. Process until smooth. Pour the mixture in an ice cube tray. Freeze and remove before the cubes are solid. Put the cubes and cream back into the food processor or blender. Blend until the mixture is thick. Pour the sorbet into a bowl and freeze until firm. Serves 6.

AVOCADO CREAM

A thick and creamy salad on ice.

1 small clove garlic
1 1/2 cups avocado, pitted and peeled
1 cup broccoli juice
1/2 cup chicken bouillon
1/2 teaspoon salt
1 tablespoon lemon juice
1/4 cup half-and-half

Put the garlic into the food processor or blender. Process until the garlic is minced. Add the avocado, broccoli juice, bouillon, salt and lemon juice. Process until smooth, but not more than 4 seconds. Pour the mixture into an ice cube tray and freeze. Remove before the cubes are solid. Put the cubes back into the food processor or blender. Add the half-and-half. Blend until the mixture is thick. Pour the sorbet into a bowl and freeze until firm. Serves 6.

TOMATO ICE

Treat yourself to this sorbet when tomatoes are in season.

1 1/2 cups tomato juice
2 tablespoons scallion juice
2 tablespoons lemon juice
2 tablespoons tomato pulp
1/2 cup water
1 clove garlic
3 tablespoons fresh basil, chopped
2 tablespoons soy sauce
1/4 teaspoon cayenne or to taste

Combine all the ingredients in a food processor or blender. Process until the garlic is minced. Pour the mixture into a cube tray and freeze. Remove before the cubes have become solid and remove the cubes. Put into a food processor and blend until the mixture has become slushy. Pour the sorbet into a bowl and freeze. Makes 6 portions.

CUCUMBER FRAPPÉ

A refreshing sorbet to serve in place of a cold soup.

1 1/2 cups cucumber juice
1/4 cup fresh parsley, coarsely chopped
2 tablespoons fresh mint, coarsely chopped
1 scallion, coarsely chopped
1/4 cup water
salt and pepper, to taste
1 cup yogurt

In a food processor or blender, combine all the ingredients except the yogurt. Process until the scallion is minced. Pour into an ice cube tray and freeze until almost solid. Remove the ice cubes. Put the ice cubes in a food processor and process until soft but not watery. Add the yogurt and process once more until well mixed. Pour the mixture into a bowl and freeze until firm. Serves 6.

Lime sorbet is a refreshing dessert after a heavy meal.

FRUITS AND VEGETABLES

APPLES

NUTRITIONAL DATA: Apples are a very good source of vitamin C. Vitamin A is present only when the skin is juiced along with the fruit. Vitamins B-1, B-2, B-6, folic and pantothenic acid are also found in lesser amounts. Potassium heads the list of minerals found in apples; found in lesser amounts are copper, magnesium and phosphorus.
USES: The vitamin and mineral content of apple juice helps to maintain the immune system against colds and the flu. The minerals are especially good in promoting healthy skin and hair. Pectin is found in a large amounts in apple juice. This substance is the same as found in over-the-counter commercial antidiarrheal medicines. High in natural sugars, apples make good juice sweeteners.
NOTES: When using apples in a juice recipe be careful to wash any possible wax from the skin. Be sure to remove the seeds before you juice. Apple seeds contain a naturally occurring cyanide/sugar compound that will deteriorate into hydrogen cyanide over time. A few seeds won't hurt you, but five or six apples' worth might make you ill. Because of apple juice's high pectin content it interferes with the body's absorption of dietary fats. Those people who have problems in digesting fats should should limit the amount of apple juice in their recipes.

ASPARAGUS

NUTRITIONAL DATA: The slender stalks of the asparagus pack a wallop of nutrition. Not only does asparagus contain large amounts of vitamins A, C, K and the B complex, but asparagus is also a good source of plant protein. Rounding out the nutritional package are the minerals iron and potassium.
USES: Asparagus juice can be used as a mild diuretic. It is safe when used in moderation. This slender plant also contains the amino acid asparagine. Asparagine is believed by some nutritionists to aid in the removal of wastes from soft tissue. This cleansing effect makes asparagus juice a perfect way regain one's balance after a binge of rich over-cooked foods.

NOTES: Vitamin K facilitates the normal clotting of human blood. Foods rich in vitamin K, like asparagus, may offset the effectiveness of anticoagulants. People taking drugs to dissolve clots and thin the blood should consult their doctors before using vitamin K-rich vegetables in their juicing recipes.

BEAN SPROUTS

NUTRITIONAL DATA: Bean sprouts contain vitamin A and the B complex of vitamins, but the B complex is less than what is found in fully mature beans. On the other hand, bean sprouts have four times the amount of vitamin A than beans. These stringy bean wannabes have a fair amount of protein and are rich in iron and potassium.
USES: Use bean sprouts as an easy mixer for most vegetable juices. They are also good in any recipe that is rich in iron, since the high vitamin C content aids in iron absorption.

BEETS

NUTRITIONAL DATA: There is an abundance of natural sugars and complex carbohydrates in beets. The real nutritive benefit from beets comes from their mineral and trace element content. Beets contain choline, iron, potassium and manganese as well as the amino acids: lysine, phenylalanine and valine. Beets also contain moderate of amounts of vitamins C and A.

USES: The amino acids and trace elements in beets make their juice a powerful blood and kidney cleanser. When mixed with high energy juices, beet juice can give that fresh ready-to-go feeling before strenuous sports activities.

NOTES: Although beet juice is known for its kidney cleansing properties, it should avoided by anyone on a strict diet to control kidney stones. Raw beets contain oxalates that can bind with calcium and can form kidney stones.

BROCCOLI

NUTRITIONAL DATA: Broccoli has as much vitamin C as fresh orange juice and as much calcium as milk. This sustaining plant is also high in vitamins A, E and K as well as such minerals as selenium and potassium. Forty-five percent of the calories in broccoli are made up of protein. But in order to utilize this protein you must mix broccoli juice with another high protein source. See NOTES.

USES: If you wish to enhance your immune system you could not find a better juice. Broccoli juice will work well in protecting the gastrointestinal and respiratory tracks from infections.

NOTES: Because the proteins found in broccoli are incomplete in their amino acid make up, it is best to combine broccoli juice with another, more complete juice, like bean sprouts. People with thyroid conditions should avoid broccoli since it contains a group of chemicals called goitorgens that may cause enlargement of the thyroid. Healthy people will not have any adverse effect. Anyone taking a test for hidden blood in the stool should not have broccoli juice within 48 hours of the test. It will produce a false positive result.

CABBAGE

NUTRITIONAL DATA: Vitamin A is found in the green patches on the cabbage leaf. The whole vegetable is rich in Vitamin C as well as moderate amounts of vitamin K, calcium, potassium and organic sulphur.

USES: Cabbage juice has a positive effect on the lower intestinal track. This cousin of the Brussel sprout also has a reputation for restoring energy and vitality, especially on the cellular level. The vitamin, mineral and trace element content of cabbage juice helps to maintain the immune system against environmental damage from industrial chemicals and cigarette smoke.

NOTES: Some people produce gas due to a bad reaction to the organic sulphur and liquified food fiber found in cabbage. In most cases just using a small amount of cabbage juice in a recipe will bypass this reaction. People with thyroid conditions should avoid cabbage since it contains a group of chemicals called goitorgens that may cause enlargement of the thyroid. Cabbage contains vitamin K and may offset the effectiveness of anticoagulants.

CARROTS

NUTRITIONAL DATA: Except for red peppers there is not another vegetable with such a high vitamin A content. In addition, carrots contain moderate amounts of the B complex and vitamin C, iodine, manganese, potassium and the amino acids arginine, hisidine, tryptophane, and valine. With such a high vitamin A content, carrots will prevent night-blindness due to vitamin A deficiency.

USES: Some nutritionists believe that drinking carrot juice on a regular basis is an excellent way to remove toxins from the liver. Carrots will also protect the larynx, esopha-

gus and respiratory track from toxic chemicals in the environment.

NOTES: It is possible to overdo a good thing. The pigments found in carrots are fat-soluble. These pigments collect in the fatty tissues just under skin. Drinking large amounts of carrot juice for more than a month will give your skin an odd yellow appearance. Carrot juice will produce a false positive result in the guiac test for hidden blood in the stool. Anyone taking such a test should not have carrot juice within 48 hours of the test.

CELERY

NUTRITIONAL DATA: Celery juice contains a moderate supply of vitamins A and C. It is rich in minerals such as calcium, manganese, potassium and organic sodium and sulphur.

USES: Because of celery juice's calcium and organic sulphur content drinking celery juice is an excellent way to aid digestion and counteract an acid stomach. Some herbalists believe that regular use of celery juice will maintain a healthy complexion. The organic sodium content of this vegetable makes celery juice a perfect mixer and natural way to add zest to your recipes.

NOTES: Use only fresh celery. Moldy or damaged stalks contain certain chemicals which may cause the skin to become painfully sensitive to light on contact.

CHERRIES

NUTRITIONAL DATA: This time consuming juice rewards the user with bountiful amounts of vitamins A, C and a lesser quantity of the B complex. Cherry juice is very rich in potassium and contains a lesser amount of cobalt, magnesium and phosphorus.

About a quarter of a cherry's weight comes from its pit and this pit must be removed before juicing, but it is well worth the effort in terms of flavor and health benefits.

USES: Herbalists use cherry juice to ease the discomfort of joint disorders as well as to reduce blood acidity.

NOTES: Be sure to remove the pit before you juice cherries. The pit contains a naturally occurring cyanide/sugar compound that will deteriorate into hydrogen cyanide over time.

CUCUMBER

NUTRITIONAL DATA: The cucumber is a member in good standing of the squash family. Although cucumbers have small amounts of the B complex and vitamin C they are very rich in minerals like calcium, magnesium, phosphorus and potassium.

USES: Cucumber juice is very, very good for the skin, hair and nails. Some nutritionists have found that drinking cucumber juice and following a moderate regimen of exercise promotes muscle flexibility. There is also a mild natural diuretic action noted with drinking cucumber juice.

NOTES: Try to buy unwaxed cucumbers. If this is not possible, and in all likelihood it is not, peel the skin before juicing. The wax which gives the cucumber its shiny appearance does not wash away with soap.

DANDELION GREENS

NUTRITIONAL DATA: Each spring homeowners fight the invasion of the dandelions. What they don't know is that this weedy intruder is also a storehouse of nutrition. Dandelion greens are packed with the B complex, vitamins A and C mixed, plus a generous amounts of calcium, iron, magnesium, phosphorus, potassium and trace elements.

USES: Dandelion greens juice has shown some effect in protecting the gastrointestinal and respiratory tracks from infections. There is also reason to believe that dandelion greens juice will offer some protection against toxic chemicals released into the environment. Because of their bitter taste, dandelion greens are best used in combination with other juices.

NOTES: Vitamin K facilitates the normal clotting of human blood. Foods like dandelion greens that are rich in vitamin K may offset the effectiveness of anticoagulants. People taking drugs to dissolve clots and thin the blood should consult their doctors before using vitamin K-rich vegetables in their juicing recipes. Dandelion greens juice contain oxalates that can bind with calcium and form kidney stones and should be avoided by anyone on a strict diet to avoid kidney stones.

GARLIC

NUTRITIONAL DATA: Garlic is high in vitamins C and B1, as well potassium, iron and selenium. Some of the potent beneficial organic compounds include allyl, disulphide allicin and alliin. This distant relative of the onion packs a culinary and nutritional punch.
USES: The compounds allicin and alliin found in garlic have been shown to have a mild antibiotic effect in laboratory and animal studies. Other studies have shown that garlic also offers some protection against circulatory diseases. Besides the aforementioned health benefits, a small amount of garlic juice will add pep to tired or mundane recipes.
NOTES: Not much garlic is needed to gain the feeling of increased vim and vigor in a matter of weeks. The only downside to using garlic on a daily basis is the possibility of garlic breath and body odor. One way to counteract this problem is to add parsley to your garlic recipes.

GRAPEFRUIT

NUTRITIONAL DATA: Like other citrus fruits, grapefruit juice contains a powerhouse of vitamin C. In addition, grapefruit juice offers fair amounts of the B complex as well as vitamins E and K. Potassium is the foremost mineral in grapefruit, followed by calcium and potassium.
USES: Daily, but moderate, intake of fresh citrus fruit juice will help to prevent colds and aid in strengthening capillary walls and healing wounds. If you drink juices rich in vitamin C along with eating foods rich in iron, the vitamin C will enhance your body's ability to absorb the iron.
NOTES: Because of its high pectin content grapefruit juice interferes with the body's absorption of dietary fats. Those people who have problems in digesting fats should should limit the amount of grapefruit juice in their recipes.

GRAPES

NUTRITIONAL DATA: Grape juice delivers moderate amounts of vitamins A, C and the B complex. Phosphorus is the main mineral found in grape juice and about 8 percent of grape juice's calories is made up of plant protein. In addition to the usual vitamin and mineral content, grape juice is rich in the natural sugars dextrose and fructose.
USES: Many European slimming diets have emphasized the use of fresh grape juice because of its natural sugars. This may seem to be a contradiction, but the theory is that the dextrose and fructose act as appetite suppressors and keep the dieter from feeling hungry during the day. Grape juice also helps to eliminate wastes and toxins from the kidneys.
NOTES: Keep grape juice in non-metal containers to prevent the juice from changing into ghastly shades of blue, purple or yellow. A little lemon or orange juice will pleasingly change red grape juice into a brighter and richer red color. Grape and grape juice fasts are popular in Swiss health spas. Care should taken not to overdo such fasts for more than one or two days without medical supervision.

JERUSALEM ARTICHOKES

NUTRITIONAL DATA: Vitamins A and C as well as the minerals calcium and potassium are found in great abundance in Jerusalem artichokes.
USES: High in natural sugars, Jerusalem artichokes make good juice sweeteners. Jerusalem artichokes are a welcome addition

Fresh asparagus appears in the spring and can be juiced into a cleansing tonic.

The most common ingredients can be juiced into vitamin-rich refreshers.

to weight gain juice recipes.

NOTES: Jerusalem Artichokes contain inulin. Some people have confused this complex and inert sugar for enzyme insulin. Inulin does not react with the human body in any way. Insulin is necessary for the sugar metabolism and can only be made by mammals, not plants. This mistake may have been due to a typographical error committed over 40 years ago, but the myth that Jerusalem Artichokes contain insulin has persisted to the present.

KALE

NUTRITIONAL DATA: Vitamin A is found in the green patches on the kale leaf. The whole vegetable is rich in Vitamin C as well as moderate amounts of vitamin K, the B complex, calcium, potassium and organic sulphur.
USES: The vitamin, mineral and trace element content of kale juice helps to strengthen the immune system against environmental damage from industrial chemicals and cigarette smoke. Kale is one of the high-alkali vegetables, good for restoring alkali-acid balance.
NOTES: Foods like kale, that are rich in vitamin K, may offset the effectiveness of anticoagulants. People taking drugs to dissolve clots and thin the blood should consult their doctors before using vitamin

K-rich vegetables in their juicing recipes. Kale juice contain a moderate amount of oxalates that can bind with calcium and form kidney stones. Caution in using this juice should be exercised by anyone on a strict diet to control kidney stones.

LEMONS AND LIMES

NUTRITIONAL DATA: Although these citrus fruits taste very different, their nutritional profile is very similar. Both lemon and lime juice have a high vitamin C content which is complemented by a fair amount of bioflavniods, potassium and calcium.
USES: A little of either one of these fruit juices adds a lot of flavor to most recipes. Both lemon and lime juice have a diuretic effect without harming the kidneys. Lemon juice was used in the nineteenth century as a natural antiseptic. French experiments showed that lemon juice killed many bacteria, including typhoid, in time periods ranging from 20 minutes to 3 hours.
NOTES: Canker sore sufferers may experience a flare-up after drinking lemon or lime juice. Avoiding these citrus juices does not prevent such attacks.

LETTUCE

NUTRITIONAL DATA: There are several types of head lettuce. Following is an aver-

age nutritional content for iceberg, romaine, Boston and leaf lettuce. In general, lettuce contains moderate to good amounts of vitamins A, K and C. Minerals range from potassium, calcium, iron and traces of iodine. Surprisingly, a moderate amount of protein can be found in most types of lettuce. Romaine lettuce has highest vitamin A content of any lettuce.
USES: Natural tranquilizers are found at the core of most head lettuce. These substances are noted for their calming effect and make good muscle relaxants.
NOTES: There is enough vitamin K in lettuce to warrant caution on the part of anyone taking anticoagulants.

MELONS

NUTRITIONAL DATA: Only the yellow melons, cantaloupe, Persian and honeydew, include vitamin A in their nutritional profile. All melons have vitamin C as well as a low amount of the B complex and high potassium content. Melon juice is a perfect summertime thirst-quencher, either chilled or at room temperature.
USES: Some nutritionists have noted a mild diuretic action associated with melon juice.
NOTES: Those people who feel bloated after eating melons following a large meal should drink melon juice on an empty stomach. This mild indigestion may be fermentation caused

by the melon juice interacting with the food in the stomach.

ORANGES

NUTRITIONAL DATA: A good deal of the vitamin C found in this citrus fruit is concentrated in the white fibrous layer that rests under the peel. In addition to containing potassium and calcium, oranges are a rich source of bioflavniods.

USES: Orange juice is a must for any tropical recipe. In fact many recipes that call for sugar, like marinades or certain sauces, can be further enhanced by substituting orange juice. In a recent survey orange was found to be America's number one flavor. Laboratory experiments with animals have shown that foods rich in bioflavniods help to keep capillaries strong and healthy. Oranges, rich in vitamin C and bioflavniods, can help speed the healing process in many people.

NOTES: Those people prone to canker sores may experience a flare-up after drinking orange juice. Avoiding orange juice does not prevent such attacks.

PAPAYAS

NUTRITIONAL DATA: Papayas are rich in vitamins A and C. They are also loaded with magnesium, phosphorus, potassium and organic sulphur.

This tropical fruit is noted for its papain content. Papain is a natural enzyme that can break down complex proteins into simple molecules. Extracted papain is the main ingredient in meat tenderizers.

USES: Rich in folk lore, papaya juice has long been used as an aid in cases of indigestion and flatulence. Papaya pulp moistened with a small amount of juice had been used in the tropics as a beauty treatment to lift dead flaky skin.

NOTES: Test a small area of the skin to see if you have an allergic reaction to papain before you use papaya juice as a beauty treatment. Anyone one taking anti-depressants or anti-hypertensives containing an MAO inhibitor must not drink papaya juice under any circumstances.

PARSLEY

NUTRITIONAL DATA: Both an herb and a vegetable, parsley contains a high quantity of vitamins A and C and a lesser quantity of thiamine, riboflavin and niacin. It is rich in such minerals as calcium, magnesium and potassium. Parsley is very rich in chlorophyll, the natural breath freshener.

USES: Parsley can be mixed in juice recipes with such odorous ingredients as garlic and onions to combat offensive breath. There are few vegetables that can match parsley juice's reputation as an overall body cleanser. It has

been used in herbal medicine as a diuretic, kidney and bladder cleanser and an immune system booster.

NOTES: Parsley juice has a very potent effect on the body: a little goes a long way. Juicing parsley concentrates all its nutrients and in liquid form it should not be used for more than three or four days in a row.

PARSNIPS

NUTRITIONAL DATA: This starchy carrot-like root is a good source of vitamin C as well as calcium and potassium. Parsnips have a strong flavor and are best used in combination with other vegetables.

USES: Any recipe with parsnip juice will enhance the nutrition needed for the good health of skin, nails and hair.

NOTES: Only use fresh parsnips. Moldy or damaged roots contain certain chemicals which may cause the skin to become painfully sensitive to light.

PEACHES

NUTRITIONAL DATA: The fuzzy peach contains a good quantity of vitamin A and fair amounts of vitamins C, B1, B2 and niacin. Calcium and potassium round out the peach's mineral content. Peach juice has been noted for its mild laxative effect when taken daily.

Papayas make wonderful juice and are not as well-known as they should be.

Melon juice combines well with berries.

USES: Potassium replacement regimens often include peaches.

NOTES: Be sure to remove the pit before you juice. Peach pits contain a naturally occurring cyanide/sugar compound that will deteriorate into hydrogen cyanide over time. A pit won't hurt you, but several might make you ill.

PEARS

NUTRITIONAL DATA: Vitamin C, a small amount of the B complex and a generous potassium content make up a pear's major nutritional profile.

USES: There is also a significant amount of fiber which is not lost in the pulp because it resides in the flesh as little gritty particles. Pear juice is very sweet and can be mixed with other fruit juices and diluted with water. The natural fiber found in pear juice makes it a good laxative. It also has a very mild diuretic effect while at the same time replacing the potassium usually lost by taking diuretics.

PINEAPPLES

NUTRITIONAL DATA: The juice of the exotic pineapple contains substantial amounts of potassium, calcium, phosphorus and organic sulphur, as well as moderate amounts of iron, and the vitamins A and C.

USES: Like the papaya, pineapples contain a natural enzyme that can break down complex proteins into simple molecules. It is called bormelain. Pineapple juice has long been used in tropical folk medicine as an all-around aid against indigestion and constipation.

NOTES: Anyone taking a test for serotonin in the urine should avoid pineapple juice for at least three days. Such tests are used to determine the presence of endocrine and gastrointestinal tumors.

PLUMS

NUTRITIONAL DATA: Vitamins A and C are found in great abundance in plum juice. Iron and potassium are found in lesser amounts. In addition to vitamin and mineral content plum juice contains a fair measure of fruit acid salts.

USES: Due to its stimulating effect on the intestines, plum juice can be used in cases of constipation and hemorrhoids.

NOTES: Be sure to remove the pit before you juice. Plum pits contain a naturally occurring cyanide/sugar compound that will deteriorate into hydrogen cyanide over time. See APPLES.

RADISHES

NUTRITIONAL DATA: Radishes, a distant cousin of the cabbage, have a healthy amount of vitamin C in addition to a moderate quantity of iron and potassium.

USES: Radish juice is usually used in combination with other vegetable juices and taken before meals for its stimulating effect on the appetite. It also has a very strong diuretic action.

NOTES: People with thyroid conditions should avoid radish juice, since it contains a group of chemicals called goitorgens that may cause enlargement of the thyroid. Healthy people will not feel any adverse effect. Anyone taking a test for hidden blood in the stool should not have radish juice within 48 hours of the test. It will produce a false positive result.

SCALLIONS

NUTRITIONAL DATA: Of all the members of onion family, scallions or green onions contain the most vitamin C and A. Scallion juice is a good source of calcium, iron, potassium and organic sulphur.

USES: Recent laboratory studies discovered that the essential oil found in scallions, and in onions generally, lower levels of LDLs (bad cholesterol) and raise levels of HDLs (good cholesterol). Scallion juice can be used as a diuretic and herbalists in Germany recommend using it as a mild anti-parasite treatment.

NOTES: Although not as strongly flavored as their rounder cousins, scallions can still cause flatulence, halitosis and indigestion in some people. Juice both green and white parts of the scallion, since each part contains a different set of nutrients.

SPINACH

NUTRITIONAL DATA: Spinach is high in vitamin C and it contains a goodly amount of vitamin A and the B complex. There is an ample quantity of phosphorus, potassium, magnesium and trace elements in spinach. It is also high in calcium, iron and protein. But these nutrients are not easily utilized by the body because the protein is considered incomplete and iron and calcium absorption is minimized by the presence of oxalic acid.
USES: It is best to use spinach juice in combination with other juices, especially if you mix it with vegetables containing protein. Spinach juice stimulates the liver and has a mild laxative effect. People taking drugs to dissolve clots and thin the blood should consult their doctors before using vitamin K-rich vegetables like spinach in their juicing recipes.
NOTES: Raw spinach contains oxalates that can bind with calcium and form kidney stones. Those people who have a tendency toward kidney stone should use spinach juice sparingly. Anyone one taking anti-depressants or anti-hypertensives containing an MAO inhibitor must not drink spinach juice under any circumstances.

STRING BEANS

NUTRITIONAL DATA: String bean juice has an ample supply of Vitamins A and C that are complemented by iodine, iron and potassium. This is not a stand-alone juice, it has an odd thick texture and must be mixed with other juices.
USES: The main reason to use string bean juice is for its bracing effect on the body's metabolism.
String bean juice will also help restore alkali balance.

SWEET PEPPERS

NUTRITIONAL DATA: Sweet peppers contain high concentrations of vitamin C and sweet red peppers have very high concentrations of vitamin A. Both red and green peppers have a good measure of iron and potassium.
USES: Pepper juice is not very appealing alone. It is very good as a flavor added to vegetable juices. Your hair, nails and skin will appreciate the addition of sweet pepper juice to your favorite juice recipes.
NOTES: Red peppers are actually mature green peppers. Vitamin A undergoes a tenfold increase during this maturation process in sweet peppers.

TOMATOES

NUTRITIONAL DATA: Tomato juice is an important source of vitamin C. There is a real difference between tomatoes grown outdoors and those that are raised in a hothouse. Hothouse tomatoes have half the vitamin C content of outdoor tomatoes. Both hothouse and outdoor tomatoes have the same amount of potassium and calcium.
USES: Eaten as a vegetable, the tomato is really a berry that is a fruit. Tomato juice is a flavorful mixer with strong flavored juices. Fresh juice is not so thick as the canned or bottled varieties and is much less acidic. Some herbalists claim that fresh tomato juice is a wonderful liver cleanser.
NOTES: Under no circumstances should you juice the leaves from vine ripened tomatoes. They contain solanine, a powerful nerve poison. Ingesting these leaves can cause illness and in great quantities, death. It is possible to overdo a good thing. The pigments found in tomatoes are fat-soluble. These pigments collect in the fatty tissues just under skin. Drinking large amounts of tomato juice for more than several weeks will give your skin an odd yellow appearance.

A WORD OF THANKS

The author would like to thank Lionel Martinez for his evocative photographs, Dr. Herbert Littlejohn for advice and information on vitamins and nutrition, the many chefs—professional and amateur—she has known and cooked with over the years, John and MaryAnn Lambert, Jane and Joe Fultz, Lee Stausland, Robin Hersha, Derek Hastings, Laura and Roger Bingham, and the staffs of AM Publishing Services and Running Press.